$300—

THE KIKKOMAN COOKBOOK

Your way to better flavor!

KIKKOMAN SHOYU CO., LTD.

Published by
Kikkoman Shoyu Co., Ltd.
1-3, Kayaba-cho, Nihonbashi, Chuo-ku, Tokyo 103, Japan
Telephone (03) 669-1111

Distributed by
Van Nostrand Reinhold Company
450 West 33rd Street
New York, NY 10001
Telephone (212) 594-8660

First printing: June 16, 1973
Second printing: June 16, 1976
Third printing: November 20, 1977

Produced by Japan Publications, Inc.
Printed in Japan.

LIBRARY OF CONGRESS CATALOG CARD NUMBER 77-26552

Preface

It makes me very happy indeed to tell you that our American plant which began production of Kikkoman Shoyu (soy sauce) in 1972 is doing quite well. We would like to take this opportunity to introduce through this book Japanese naturally-brewed shoyu.

It is said that shoyu had its beginning in Japan more than one thousand years ago when the idea of fermenting soybeans was introduced from China. Over the centuries since that time, shoyu has been developed to suit the Japanese environment and people. The Japanese genius for attention to detail and for working in harmony with nature have brought shoyu to the peak of perfection as the unique, all-purpose seasoning. In other words, shoyu is a masterpiece of flavor and taste, perfected through cooperation of men and beneficient nature over many centuries.

With this tradition as a background, Kikkoman has, for the past 400 years, endeavored to bring to all consumers "a better product, at a lower price, in greater abundance." As a result, people in nearly 100 countries now treasure and use Kikkoman shoyu. Among these countries America is the largest overseas market. In fact, Americans have come to appreciate Kikkoman shoyu so much that a shoyu production plant in America itself is economically the most feasible way to bring our product to the American consumer.

In the fields of politics and economics, there have been, in the past, many barriers to human communication. In the world of flavor, however, we are demonstrating that there are no national boundaries. People all over the world, we believe, will appreciate something delicious entirely on its own merits. Therefore in the future we fully intend to continue devoting our every effort to serving people everywhere; to help make eating a richer, more pleasurable experience for people all over the world.

We have prepared this book, in the hope that it will help deepen your understanding of shoyu, your enjoyment of foods seasoned with shoyu, and beyond that, your understanding of one important aspect of Japanese culture.

I would like to express my sincere appreciation to everyone concerned for taking time from their busy schedules to help make this book possible. A special word of thanks must go to Dr. Shigeru Otsuka, Professor at Toyo Junior College of Food Technology, who wrote the first part of the book, to Mrs. E. T. Beatson for her creative recipes, to the editors, Mr. Toyoshima and Miss Kubota of Japan Publications, to Mr. W. Hessling for his translation, and all others who cooperated so wholeheartedly in the project.

November, 1977

Keizaburo Mogi
Chairman, Kikkoman Shoyu Co., Ltd.

Contents

Preface . . . . *by* Keizaburo Mogi. 3
Contents

All ABOUT SHOYU . . . . *by* Shigeru Otsuka. 7

Shoyu and Japanese Food 8
    Japanese Cuisine Defeated? 8
    The Europeans Come to Japan 10
Japanese Food and Nature 11
Shoyu and Nature 13
The Japanization of Western Food 15
The Basic Role of Shoyu in Japanese Cooking 16
The History of Shoyu 18
    Fermentation and Taste 18
    Commercial Production 20
    Shoyu and the West 20
Shoyu Production Process 22
    Shoyu Production Process 22
    Raw Materials 23
    Koji Making 24
    Fermentation and Brewing 25
    Pressing 25
Shoyu Components 26
    The Components of Bouquet 26
    Flavor Components 27
    The Coloring of Shoyu 27
Shoyu and Cooking 28
Shoyu and Health: Japanese Cooking, a Healthy Diet 29
    Shoyu is "digested soybean protein" 29
    Taste and Digestion 29
    Tastiness Versus Fat (Japanese Cooking Versus Western Cooking) . . 29
Conclusion: Shoyu Is for All Mankind 33

RECIPES WITH BREWED SOY SAUCE
    from the Kikkoman Cooking Center and *Kikkoman Cook Book* 34

Appetizers 34
    Menehune Chicken 34
    Chicken Kabobs (Yakitori) 34
    Chinese Barbecued Pork (Char Siu) 36
    Mushroom Hors d'oeuvres 36
    California Beef Jerky 37
    Curry Dip 38
    Sesame Dip 38
    Western Nuts & Eastern Bolts 38
Salads and Salad Dressing 39
    Oriental Cucumber Salad (Sunomono) 39
    Celery Victor 39
    Salad "Nice" Style 40
    Vinaigrette Salad Dressing 41
Beef 42
    Beef Sukiyaki 42
    Sukiyaki—A "Japanese" Dish Coming Home to the West 44
    Beef Tatsuta Style 42
    Shabu-shabu 45
    Shoyu-Pickled Beef 46
    Flank Steak 47
    Swiss Steak Teriyaki 47
    Lemony Beef Kabobs 47
    Kauai Beef Kabobs 48
    Mushroom Burgers 48
    Sloppy Joes 50
    Madhatter Meatballs 50
    Teriyaki Meat Loaf 51
    Barbecued Short Ribs 51
Chicken and Egg 52
    Crispy Oven-Fried Chicken 52
    Chicken In A Basket 52
    Barbecued Chicken Filled Korean Style 52
    Chicken-Cashew Nut Saute 54
    Gourmet Chicken 55
    Chicken Confetti 55
    Chicken Venetian 55
    "Come Again" Chicken 56
    Sauce and Bake Chicken 57
    Simple Skillet Chicken Teriyaki 58
    Stuffed Eggs 58

Pork and Lamb 59
    Glazed Pork Chops 59
    Braised Island Pork 59
    Pork Cutlets Milano Style. 60
    Sweet-Sour Pork 61
    Spareribs Hawaiian 62
    Sweet-Sour Spareribs 62
    Barbecued Spareribs 64
    Lazy-Day Lamb Pilaf 64
    Broiled Lamb Chops 65
    Lamb Spareribs 65
Sea Food 66
    Seafood and Vegetable Tempura. 66
    Tempura—A "Japanese" Dish Imported From the West 68
    Shrimp-Curl Kabobs 67
    Prawns in the Shell 69
    Scallop Casserole 69
    Tuna Casserole 70
Sauces. 71
    All-purpose Seafood Sauce 71
    Basic Teriyaki Sauce 71
    Western Barbecue Sauce 72
    Zesty Steak Sauce 72
    Asparagus with Peanut Butter-shoyu Sauce 72
    Tangy Dipping Sauce for Vegetables 73
    Quick and Zesty Topping for Vegetables 73
Miscellaneous 74
    Hawaiian Ham Steak 74
    Corn-on-the-cob Kikkoman 74
    Celery Kikkoman 74
Japanese Cooking 76
    Nigiri Sushi 76
    Chirashi Sushi. 77
    Suimono (Clear Soup) 78
    Udon 79

Postscript . . . . *by* Saheiji Mogi 80

All ABOUT SHOYU*

by Shigeru Otsuka

Professor at Toyo Junior College of Food Technology

Some years ago a man won first prize in a Chicago steak-broiling contest. His steak looked exactly like any other steak, but he had just one secret: a little shoyu, only a dash, to bring out the true goodness of the beef.

The story behind the story was that during his military service he had been stationed in Japan. While there, something happened that was to change his life; he tried sukiyaki and was entranced by the deep, rich tastiness of not only the meat, but the vegetables and other ingredients as well. Upon investigation and a little thought, he soon realized that the secret was in the use of shoyu. His enthusiasm grew as he studied more about this extraordinary seasoning, and after his return to America he continued to develop his use of shoyu as part of his professional know-how.

In 1969 Radio WOR of New York held a contest for the best " recipe using shoyu." Of the 1200 entrants, first prize went to Miss Hyla Snider of Quaker Hill, Connecticut for her shrimp teriyaki recipe.

More and more American consumers are beginning to recognize that this Far Eastern seasoning can do good things for their own favorite dishes. Take for example my English teacher, Father Dennis, who counts cooking and magic among his many accomplishments. Although he had lived in Japan more than ten years, he had never really gotten on speaking terms with shoyu, since he seldom ate out. He cooked all his own food and, being a bit on the conservative side, this was limited to the foods he had liked in his native St. Louis. Not long ago he took a trip home, where he stayed at his sister's house. One night at dinner, as he was launching into an explanation of Japanese food, he noticed his little nephew shaking some kind of dark liquid onto his food from a small dispenser bottle. He asked what it was, and his nephew, rather surprised, replied, "It's Japanese shoyu. Don't you know what shoyu is?" "Yes, I know what it is, but . . . do you like it?" "Sure, it makes everything taste better. It's just like your magic."

With that, Father Dennis's discourse on Japanese food somehow just couldn't quite regain its former momentum.

So it would appear that shoyu has gone a long way toward gaining a definite position in the everyday eating habits of the American people. In kitchens and on dinner tables throughout the country, salt, pepper and catchup are moving over to

NOTE: I have chosen to use the name "shoyu" instead of "soy sauce", "soy" or "soya" because, frankly, I don't like any of these English names; they have come to refer to various chemically-made versions of the original naturally-brewed seasoning.

make room for this newcomer from Japan. More and more Americans are "discovering" shoyu, as one housewife told me she had done at Osaka's Expo '70.

"Discovered?" Amused and bemused, I turned this idea over in my mind. After all, if from their viewpoint Europeans can say Columbus "discovered" the western hemisphere even though the Indians had lived there for thousands of years, then perhaps we can say that shoyu has been discovered by the Americans. Without losing sight of the fact that shoyu has been used in Japan for nearly 1000 years, however.

On the other hand, I'm sorry to have to say that present-day Americans are not the first Westerners to discover shoyu. Three hundred years ago in France, Louis XIV imported Japanese shoyu as a secret seasoning to be used in the foods served at his sumptuous palace dinners. So after all, it would seem that the title "Discoverer of Shoyu" must go to Louis XIV. And, of course, to the Japanese who, for hundreds of years before that time, had used shoyu to the best advantage in developing elegant Japanese cuisine.

Shoyu and Japanese Food

Japanese Cuisine Defeated?

The defeat of Japanese cuisine, according to some Japanese scholars, can be blamed on shoyu. Let's see what they mean.

Over the last 100 years of fierce international competition, it is said, Japanese cuisine has been thoroughly bested by Western and Chinese food. Take America for example. America has been called a melting pot of peoples. With people coming from all countries of the world, America also inevitably served as a world test kitchen, and in fact still does. Americans, when they take foreign visitors out for dinner, will ask their guests what national dishes they prefer. In this respect Americans are said to be unique. People of other countries naturally tend to take foreign visitors to taste the best of their own national food. But most Americans will ask, "Shall we make it Chinese food? Italian? Or how about some French food?"

This is because there is nothing that we can clearly identify as "American cuisine." People from many countries of greatly differing culinary habits have come together over the past 450 years in the great effort of nation-building on this new continent. To some extent the people themselves have blended through intermarriage, but their eating habits have stubbornly resisted change. Which is not really so surprising because, as most specialists in the study of national customs maintain, among the three necessities of life, food, clothing and shelter, food habits are the most conservative and resistant to change.

So the many national cuisines failed to blend and form an "American cuisine." Some people say that the hamburger and the hotdog make up the true American cuisine, but probably not many readers would go along with this. Rather, what has emerged from the American culinary-historical experience is a number of culinary groups. These groups, which are a mixture of such widely differing elements as "just-like-my-grandma-made-it" innocence and super-sophisticated French court cuisine, are the "French food," "Chinese food," "Italian food," and "Scandinavian food" presently found in America.

Please notice that Japanese cuisine did not receive the distinction of being numbered among the groups that thus managed to remain in America. You may say that this is because there were too few Japanese in the United States, but that theory doesn't hold water. By 1940 there were 1.5 times as many Japanese as Chinese in America. But Chinese restaurants are to be found in even small towns in all parts of the United States. Moreover, they are patronized almost exclusively by non-Chinese Americans. Japanese restaurants, on the other hand, are virtually non-existent except for the West Coast and New York. Further, until very recently customers of such Japanese restaurants were almost all gastonomically homesick Japanese, or occasional Americans invited there by Japanese friends. These non-Japanese guests would typically express amazement at each dish brought before them, and would approach the task of actually eating the stuff very gingerly indeed.

On the other hand Chinese food, which of course is also Far Eastern, which also includes relatively large amonts of seafood, and which also involves using chopsticks, has staked out a firm position for itself in America as a special culinary treat, while Japanese food has been considered merely exotic at best, or grotesque and distasteful at worst.

No doubt this American evaluation represents the entire world in expressing the defeat of Japanese cuisine in international competition. Certainly there is no mistaking the fact that the Japanese cuisine has utterly failed to spread to other parts of the world.

Then there was the military defeat of Japan itself in 1945, a defeat which gave the coup de grâce to Japanese cuisine on the international front. Since then Japanese food has been making a little progress, thanks to the post-war American military occupation, the Korean War, the Viet Nam War, the Tokyo Olympic Games and Osaka's Expo '70.

Why has Japan's cuisine been so singularly unsuccessful internationally? The most likely theory is the one that places the blame on shoyu. The reason is simple in the extreme: shoyu is entirely too good. Therefore the Japanese people, including the top chefs, have failed to develop individual sauces to complement the different basic materials. They have not bothered to really think about better methods of preparation. Instead, they have been content to season everything with only one seasoning—shoyu.

And to be sure, shoyu does make everything taste better—meat, fish, poultry and vegetables. A dash of shoyu in soup or boiled dishes brings out the natural flavor in a way that is nothing short of fantastic.

As a matter of fact, there are quite a few foods that just aren't very good until shoyu does its thing with them. For example, eels. In many European countries eel soup is commonly served. Even the most avid European gastronomic nationalist would be hard-pressed to honestly call this soup really tasty or of a high culinary level. But seasoned with a shoyu-base marinade eels become kabayaki (eel teriyaki), one of Japan's finest dishes, and a Far Eastern delicacy that Western people cannot forget once they have tasted it.

Or take seaweed, which is gaining a reputation now in America as a health food effective in preventing high blood pressure and obesity. Japanese people have long been fond of seaweed, but without shoyu to season it even the Japanese would never have come to eat seaweed nor, of course, to pass it on to the rest of the world.

So if the defeat of Japanese cuisine has some relation with shoyu, I think we can say the fault lies in the overdependence of Japanese culinary leadership on the goodness of shoyu. The goodness of shoyu, and the ability of shoyu to complement any kind of food, are the virtues of shoyu, and I for one would hesitate to lay any harsh blame on it for being too good. After all, just because a beautiful woman is the cause of a crime by another, we can hardly say she is to blame for the crime by reason of being beautiful.

The Europeans Come to Japan

Europeans first came to Japan and tasted Japanese food in the middle of the 16th century. First was a group of Portuguese who had set out for China in search of Far Eastern spices. They landed on an island called Tanegashima near the southernmost tip of Japan. Six years later a group of missionaries headed by St. Francis Xavier arrived in Kyoto, at that time the capital of Japan.

These missionaries seem to have suffered considerably because of their diet while in Japan. One of the group wrote in a letter home, "In this country there is no olive oil, butter, cheese, milk, eggs, sugar, honey or vinegar, nor is there to be found any saffron, bay leaves, or pepper. But even with this simple food the people here are wonderfully healthy, and the number of old people is amazing."

While he was mistaken in his belief that there were no eggs, sugar or vinegar, as for the other items there was indeed none at all or very little of them in the Japan of that time.

Oil, butter, cheese and milk are Western foods, and at the same time are important seasonings in a great many Western sauces and soups. Lacking these as well as spices such as saffron, bay and pepper, the early missionaries must have been completely unable to season their foods as they were accustomed to doing. Even Xavier, who was one of the founders of the Jesuit order, rather inscrutably proclaimed, "God has granted us a grace by leading us to a country where we cannot indulge in luxuries."

No, there was no animal fat to be had, neither beef nor pork, no vegetable oil, no milk. But in the Japan of that time there was shoyu. It was the great misfortune of the Portuguese that they did not know it. The Dutch traders that followed them, however, did notice shoyu, and began to export it to Europe. It was about 100 years later that Lóuis XIV of France began to prize shoyu as a secret ingredient in the luxurious court fare of the time.

Japanese Food and Nature

Imagine the United States, with the north-south axis as is but with the east-west axis shrunk to 1/10 its present width, leaving the land along the Atlantic coast, bordered on the west by the Appalachian Range. Then cut it into four large islands and thousands of smaller islands. From the state of Maine to the Florida peninsula there is a great variety of fruits and vegetables, and in the surrounding ocean and bays, from near-arctic to near-tropical, a great wealth of seafood. More-over, this long slender group of islands is strongly influenced by the surrounding seas, giving it at least four clearly differentiated seasons. The continuous change and interplay of these seasons influence the living things, evolving many clearly divided species of plants and animals.

Foods differ completely according to place and season. It is one of the joys of living in this land to observe the fruits and vegetables and fish in the local shops as they parade their many colors in unending seasonal change. Even the taste of the same variety of fish differs according to the season. Most fish are fattest and taste best before the season for laying their eggs. This season differs according to species, so it is possible to enjoy fish at their very best all year long. The same holds true for fruit and vegetables. And even though this land may be lacking in foods that are available throughout the year, such as meat, poultry, eggs and milk, still the tables of the people living here are decorated with something new and different all through the year. Indeed, in such a country it is the dinner tables of the people that show most clearly the change of the seasons. It is on their tables that Nature shows herself in her myriad shapes and colors. In such a country the people have an exchange of courtesies with Nature that is unknown and unknowable to people who make their homes on vast continents.

This land is Japan. Because the many seasonal foods in this land change at such a dizzying pace, there is more than enough variety throughout the year even supposing there were no additional variety provided by different methods of cooking. For example, even if we were to limit our methods of preparing fish to one, say grilling over an open fire, in the course of a year we would be able to enjoy more than 30 different eating experiences. Multiply these by other preparation methods such as sashimi, teriyaki, tempura, boiled fish dishes and so on, and you can see that there is very little reason to suffer from lack of variety. Nor is there any need in this land to depend on any one basic food, for example beef, or to think up different ways of presenting such a single basic food in pleasing variety, or to worry about methods of storage.

This is the kind of environment that brought forth Japanese cuisine. In Japan the people highly value the natural coloring, shape, taste and aroma of foods, and they add only a bare minimum of flavoring to their foods, preferring to maintain as much as possible the natural goodness, texture and feeling of the materials them-selves. The skill of a cook is in fact judged by how well he succeeds in bringing out the natural flavor of his materials. A professional cook in Japan is carefully trained in artistic cutting of his materials, and in arranging them attractively on plates.

In old 'Japan, a cook was called a "slicer man," meaning a man who used a slicing knife professionally. Even now the Japanese say of a cook that he can get by in the world with only his trusty slicing knife. It is something like the samurai in olden days who would wander throughout the country with only his beloved sword as companion, always in search of a challenge, or, in the European experience, like a violinist who might wander about in search of a master-teacher, his precious violin always in his hand; so a cook, with his slicer honed to razor sharpness, would roam from town to town, always practicing, always looking for someone who could teach him something new in the preparation of food.

It has been said that Japanese cuisine is "food to be looked at." The many plates and bowls are tastefully arranged on an elegant table, with the food itself arranged with such careful attention to form and color harmony that it seems a shame to destroy the beauty merely in order to eat the food. Americans often remark that such dishes seem to them more works of art than food. But while from the point of view of the eater it may be "food to be looked at," from the viewpoint of the cook it is "food that took a lot of expert cutting." We can understand this more clearly when we consider that the English verb "cook" means mainly the operation involving the application of heat, and cutting is nothing more than a preparatory operation. On the other hand, the corresponding Japanese verb "ryori suru" includes three concepts, the cutting of the materials, the application of heat, and the artistic arrangement for serving, with equal emphasis on each of the three.

We can say that the method of food preparation is one of the most characteristic aspects of a people's culture. Therefore there is an intimate connection between the classification of food preparation and human culture. At present, the world can be divided into four large groups, the European, the Arab/Turk, the Indian, and the Chinese. Japan of course falls in the Chinese group.

However, as I have mentioned before, Japan as an island country has taken quite an individual course of cultural development. Unlike China, Japan has no tradition of using large amounts of pork or oils. Rather, the Japanese much prefer fresh fish and vegetables. So in many important respects Japanese food has over the last 400 years become separated from the Chinese group of food preparation.

There is one more thing that must be mentioned concerning the influence that Nature exerts over a nation's eating habits: Nature in a warm, rainy island country in the temperate zone is the friend of the people who live there. In the fields there are always delicious plants for them to eat, and birds and small animals, and many kinds of fish in the surrounding seas.

Even the mountains in such a land extend a warm welcome to mankind. Winter may be cold, but from spring through autumn the mountain herbs and vegetables, the fruits of trees and bushes, and the animal life provide abundant fare for the table. And with just a little cultivation a bountiful harvest can be taken.

In Japan there is a long tradition of "living the life of a hermit," and of "giving up the world and living in the mountains." In fact there have been many historical cases of people in Japan who had come to view human relations with distaste, or had become sickened with civilization, and chose to lead a completely secluded life. What made such a choice possible was the abundance of food provided by Nature in Japan's hospitable mountains. This is quite a different situation from that of China or Europe, with their inhospitable continental climates, where people feel the need to cluster close together for comfort and safety, where at times they even feel the need to build high walls around their cities for protection. In such lands Nature must be an implacable foe of man in some respects.

Nature was a friend to the Japanese, always giving food to them in abundance, as well as spiritual sustenance. Most Zen temples were deep in the mountains. The spirit of Zen could be summarized as "reverence for Buddha and Nature". Indeed, the ordinary people themselves were a part of Nature and lived as such in Japan. The fact that in Japanese haiku poetry and in Japanese painting man is clearly perceived as only a part of Nature rather than as the central subject of art clearly illustrates this traditional Japanese attitude toward human life in its relationship to Nature.

But unfortunately, since joining the family of modern nations about 100 years ago, Japan has rejected Nature and has imitated the West in developing a machine civilization and, through an unnatural (for Japanese) affirmation of the man-made, Japan is now despoiling its beautiful mountains and plains and befouling the environment with the vile effluvients of industrialization. At present Japan's natural environment is being destroyed at a rate which is among the fastest in the world. But I will refrain from delving into that subject here. I only want to be sure that you understand that until the end of the 19th century most Japanese lived in friendship and harmony with Nature, and that their culinary life too was essentially integrated with Nature.

Shoyu and Nature

As we have seen, the Japanese lived in close harmony with Nature and rejoiced in the bounty of Nature—the bounty of the ocean depths, the abundance of the mountain fastness—but here we run straight into a problem. The fact is, and it almost makes one think that God made a slight slip in the act or creation, that Nature's food taken straight is not really very tasty. And taste becomes an increasingly important factor in the enjoyment of food when people reach a certain level of affluence and civilization. The seasoning of food then becomes the first step in its preparation.

The word "seasoning," incidentally, most likely came from "to adapt for the season" (or seasonal natural foods).

No doubt salt was the first seasoning used by man. However, salt alone as a seasoning, especially in the case of foods having very little fat, is entirely too harsh on the tongue to give proper seasoning to foods.

Perhaps you have heard of "honeymoon salad" which is made using only lettuce with salt sprinkled over it—lettuce alone without dressing! It doesn't even make a very good pun, let alone a good salad. And the reason it would not make a good salad, why you would never find such a salad on a honeymoon hotel menu, is that the taste would certainly bear no resemblance to the soft, sweet mellowness of the ideal honeymoon. Lettuce contains almost no oils, and salt alone on it would be harsh indeed to the tongue.

Now the origin of the words "salad" and "salt" are said to be the same, coming from an early custom of seasoning vegetables with salt. It would seem, however, that salt alone left something to be desired. And so oil or dressing containing oil came to be the usual companion to salad.

Later I will discuss the role that oil or fat plays in mellowing the taste of salt (see "Shoyu and Health"). In the case of Japan, where not much oil or fat is used, the method chosen to improve upon Nature and at the same time emphasize natural flavor was shoyu.

Shoyu contains about 18% salt, but when you pour a little out and taste it, it does not taste nearly that salty. This has been called one of the seven wonders of shoyu, and it is caused mainly by the action of amino acids that make the saltiness mild to the tongue. As a test, take an 18% salt water solution, (six times the salinity of sea water) and compare the taste with that of shoyu. It is the action of micro-organisms that produces amino acids in shoyu. In other words, shoyu is a product of nature.

Already in the time of the *Tale of Genji*—some 1200 to 1300 years ago— something very like modern day shoyu had become in indispensable element of the aristocratic banquets of that age. At present in Japan shoyu is used freely both in the kitchen and at the table, but according to earliest records it seems to have been used chiefly at the table, and was listed on menus of the day along with salt and vinegar. To be sure, we can say that this early shoyu must have been far from a perfected product, and that it was not very good-tasting. In fact, while we can say that there were certain elements of Japanese cooking already perfected at this time, the conpletion of the national cuisine as we now know it would have to await the further development of cooking methods, the perfection of shoyu, and the importation of foreign elements and techniques.

A little before this time there was a development that was to deeply influence, we should even say shape, the Japanese eating habits. This was the introduction of Buddhism. By decrees of devout Buddhist Emperors the eating of animal meat was forbidden. This ban continued until modern times, which meant that the Japanese cuisine grew up with fish, shellfish, poultry, fruits, vegetables and seaweed as its main items.

The Japanization of Western Food

Into this milieu came the contact with Chinese and European foods in the 14th and 15th centuries.

Especially revolutionary was the coming of the Portuguese and Dutch in the 14th century, and then the contacts made with Americans and with Western eating habits and foods in the last half of the 19th century. Revolutionary, it must be said, for both the Japanese people and for their cooking. With the eagerness of the true eclectic, the Japanese welcomed new and exotic ideas along with the new foods from across the sea.

There is one special aspect of this enrichment of the Japanese cuisine that is especially noteworthy. This is the fact that no matter how eagerly the Japanese took in Western foods, they never accepted Western customs and habits of eating. Instead they incorporated the foods into their own customs and created a Japanized style of Western food. This was done chiefly through the use of shoyu. To see just how successfully this was done, let us look at one example, sukiyaki.

The first time the common people in Japan had seen beef in more than 1000 years was a scant 100 years ago. And the first time they picked up beef in their hands and looked at it, the first time they worked up enough courage to actually eat it, it was not as beefsteak or as roast beef. Instead they sliced it very thin and boiled it with vegetables and tofu. That was the start of sukiyaki. Thin-slicing was the same method they had used to prepare raw fish for over a thousand years. And cooking it at the table seasoned with shoyu was none other than the method they had long used to prepare their fish and poultry dishes. Now, a century later, of all typically Japanese dishes sukiyaki is the undoubted favorite among Europeans and Americans.

Going back a little earlier for another example, tempura was introduced into Japan in the 17th century. The deep-frying method used for tempura was quite a revolutionary thing to the Japanese of the time. The word "tempura" is said to be a corruption of either a Spanish or a Portuguese word. As we can judge by the choice of a foreign word for this new dish, the Japanese of that age must have considered such food exotic indeed.

Here again in the case of tempura we can see that the new food became truly Japanese only after the perfection of a shoyu-base sauce, "ten-tsuyu," to go with it. And of course tempura was developed using traditional Japanese materials: fish, shrimp, shellfish and vegetables. Now tempura is among the few Japanese dishes that have won truly wide acceptance internationally.

In the case of other "foreign foods" as well, for example, Chinese dishes, breaded cutlets, and many others, shoyu-base sauces have been the key to their development in Japan.

Yes, when the Japanese come upon some new food, their first impulse is to sprinkle it with shoyu or cook it in shoyu. Onions, Chinese cabbage, spinach, Irish potatoes, carrots, tomatoes, eggplant, cabbage, all have either come to Japan, or have come to by widely eaten, within the last century, and all of them have come to be appreciated when seasoned and cooked with shoyu.

Actually, this phenomenon is not limited to foods and food preparation methods imported from abroad. Sashimi, the Japanese raw fish delicacy, was eaten as a vinegared fish salad for more than 1000 years, but it became a really popular dish among the Japanese only after the present method of dipping the raw fish slices in shoyu was devised a mere 200–300 years ago.

The Basic Role of Shoyu in Japanese Cooking

It is commonly said that most Japanese foods include shoyu. I would say rather that shoyu is used in some form in virtually all Japanese cooking. Basically Japanese cooking is no different from any other kind of cooking in that it consists mainly of raw dishes, broiled dishes, boiled dishes, deep fried dishes, etc. However, the distinctive "tastiness," aroma and color of shoyu are used to give a salty taste in some cases, a special delicious aroma in other situations, and sometimes a few drops of soy sauce are used in what the Japanese call "subtle seasoning".

The use of shoyu in Japanese cooking can be outlined as:

(1) *Broiled fish:*
Shoyu is often used to add a special deliciousness to broiled fish dishes.

(2) *Boiled fish:*
Fish is boiled for 15 to 20 minutes over a low flame in a mixture of shoyu, sugar and water. Care should be taken to remove the fish from the mixture before it begins to fall to pieces.

(3) *Vegetables and meat:*
Selected vegetables are boiled in water containing sugar and salt until they become tender. A touch of shoyu is added after boiling.

(4) *Noodles:*
Boiled noodles are sometimes dipped in a shoyu-base soup and eaten cold. At other times the noodles are heated and added to the soup and chicken or deep fried fish and vegetables (tempura) are added to the dish just before eating.

(5) *Sauces:*
Shoyu-base sauces are made for dipping and grilling different foods. These sauces are applied to the food before, during and after grilling. More recently ready-made sauces have been put on the market. Usually the food is marinated in this sauce for some time before it is grilled. Depending on the food, the sauce may also be brushed on the food lightly after it has been grilled to some degree. This sauce can also be used for boiled fish dishes.

(6) *Mixtures:*

When shoyu and vinegar are mixed their respective tastes complement each other and blend into a delicious sauce. This sauce can be used to season boiled vegetables. Sugar is often added to this sauce.

A dip made by mixing sour-tasting citrus fruit juices with shoyu is used for dipping boiled foods. This dip is also used for steamed and deep-fried dishes. A dip made from grated ginger and shoyu is also used with many kinds of foods.

(7) *Soup*

Japanese soup is different from European and American soups in that it is not made from the broth of boiled chicken, etc. Typical Japanese soup uses shoyu and bean paste as a soup base. Vegetables, fish and meat are added to give body to these soups.

Sometimes grated dried bonito, dried mushrooms and dried seaweed are boiled and the stock is used as a base for Japanese soups, or added to boiled vegetable soups. Chemical seasonings such as monosodium glutamate, sodium inosinate and sodium guanilate are also used in soup bases in Japan. All of these additions are used to bring out the taste in Japanese food and are generally considered indispensable to Japanese cooking.

(8) *Subtle seasoning:*

Of course there are some Japanese dishes in which shoyu is not used or in which the taste of shoyu is not evident. However, even in these cases a few drops of shoyu are generally added to the dish. But these few drops of shoyu make a surprising difference in the taste. The Japanese call this technique "subtle seasoning".

(9) *Pickled vegetables:*

The aroma and taste of shoyu is also complementary to pickled vegetables. The greatest variety of pickled vegetables in the world is found in Japan and shoyu is used for seasoning in practically all varieties.

The History of Shoyu

Fermentation and Taste

As is evident from the English name "soy sauce", the main ingredient of shoyu is soybeans. The end product, however, does not have a soybean taste or smell. Naturally tomato sauce has the aroma of tomatoes, white sauce has the aroma of milk and anchovy sauce has the aroma of anchovies. However, in the case of "soy sauce" the same is not true. In other words, why is it that shoyu has a special aroma and taste which is not found in the soybean? The answer to this riddle is found in the fermentation process. A different section is dedicated to a detailed explanation of the fermentation process, so here it will suffice to say that the same phenomenon is evident in cheese and tea. In the case of cheese and tea, the end products have an entirely different taste and aroma from the original milk and tea leaves.

Due to the action of microorganisms during the fermentation process, many different materials are broken down and are changed into other materials. Men have been using this process to make wine, beer, vinegar, cheese, yogurt and other products since time immemorial. More recently the fermentation process has been used to make glycerine, citric acid, lactic acid, vitamin B2, vitamin C, penicillin, and streptomycin. In fact this process is used to make everything from chemicals to medicine.

The fermentation process is basically a result of the action of mold, yeast and bacteria. The mild damp climate of Japan is ideal for the growth of these three types of organism, a fact which, no doubt, contributed greatly to the early development of sake, miso, shoyu, vinegar and other products of fermentation. This natural advantage of climate, in fact, has helped Japan to become a leader in the modern fermentation industry.

When things which have a high protein content such as meat, soybeans, etc. are steeped in a salty liquid, the protein is broken down and turns into amino acid. This amino acid is instrumental in activating human taste buds and giving a pleasurable sense of tastiness. This phenomenon has apparently been known for many centuries in China and South East Asia, where it has been used to make a salty liquid seasoning for vegetables and soup.

A similar salty liquid had probably long been known in Japan too. However, the production of the forerunner of modern shoyu was not started in Japan until around the 7th century. At that time the Emperor of Japan issued an edict forbidding the use of meat. As a result of this edict the process used in the production of this salty liquid seasoning, the fermenting of soybeans, was introduced from China. The introduction of this process to Japan was the first step in the development of shoyu as we know it today. From that time forward the Japanese devoted themselves to

Hiroshige print showing shoyu making (19th century)

improving shoyu. By the beginning of the 8th century the forerunner of modern shoyu had already become an important form of seasoning in Japan. At that time more than 10 different kinds of shoyu-type seasonings were being produced in Japan and it is thought that an approximation of modern shoyu was eventually arrived at in the 14th century as a result of a trial and error process. By the 14th century, Japanese shoyu had become superior to both the Chinese and Korean varieties. In 1775 a Swedish doctor and botanist named Thunberg came to Japan and reported in a book called "Travels in Japan" that the Japanese variety of shoyu was far superior to that produced in China. He also wrote a commentary on the process used in shoyu production in Japan.

The process used in the production of the forerunner of shoyu in Japan developed along independent lines and is now used in making "miso." (miso is a paste made from soy beans and rice or other grains, and is extensively used as a seasoning for soup.) In this way a superior quality "miso" was also developed in Japan.

The greatest difference between shoyu and other seasonings is that shoyu has been mostly sold as a finished product almost from the time it began to be developed. Other seasonings have been made in the home until quite recently. Even in the case of "miso" the same is true. At present most of the miso produced in Japan is produced in factories but there are still instances where housewives in rural communities make it by themselves. They usually make a year's supply at one time. In comparison, shoyu which is made in the home is a rarity. The reason is that shoyu has a very delicate taste which can be ruined by a small variation in temperature, etc. and consequently is very difficult to produce in the home. Even experts must take great care in producing this delicate taste.

Shoyu is different from a salted broth made with fish or meat in that it not only has a very delicious taste but also has a full bodied aroma and color.

Shoyu is not something that can be improved by improvising; like fine wine or high quality beer, shoyu is a completely natural and honest product which cannot be tampered with.

Commercial Production

It is said that shoyu was first commercially produced in a place called Yuasa near Osaka in 1290. In the middle of the 16th century commercial production was started in Noda near Tokyo.

After many years of quality-related competition between various shoyu makers, Noda finally won out as the principal shoyu producing center for the important urban market of Edo (the present-day Tokyo).

Noda continued as the "Shoyu town" of the Tokyo area, with numerous family-owned companies competing for a market share. After centuries of operating in the same line of business all these families were related by intermarriage and at last in 1917 the eight largest companies merged to form the Noda Shoyu Company, now known as Kikkoman Shoyu Co., Ltd.

Shoyu and the West

While shoyu was thus developing and maintaining its relationship with Japanese culinary arts, it was also the object of strong foreign interest on at least two occasions.

The first of those was in the middle of the 17th Century when shoyu was exported from Nagasaki by the Dutch. At the time, Japan was following a policy of national isolationism, and foreign intercourse or trade were prohibitted by the Shogun. It was only at Nagasaki that this prohibition was relaxed slightly and trade in a few limited items continued. Holland was one of the three most active nations in Europe, along with Spain and Portugal, during that period.

And for the Japanese, Nagasaki was adrift in an exotic European or Chinese atmosphere non-existent elsewhere in Japan. Although the period was somewhat different, this Nagasaki was the setting for the love story of a geisha in the opera "Madame Butterfly".

Shoyu was thus exported to Ceylon and India and, through the Dutch, was carried into Europe. There it was used as a "secret flavor" in the feasts prepared in the kitchens of the opulent Court of Louis XIV of France, as related earlier. Shoyu was an expensive, even precious, commodity and cuisine utilizing shoyu was a matter of pride to the chefs of the European nobility.

A much more recent connection was around 1947. At the end of World War II there was a scarcity of soybeans and Japan had to depend primarily on soybeans grown in America. The allotment of soybeans to individual shoyu makers was carried out by the Occupation office in charge of economic and scientific afairs. The official in charge of shoyu was a Miss Appleton, whose knowledge of the flavor and the position of shoyu in Japan was incomplete. She considered only the time required for the preparation and processing of the raw materials (ordinary brewed shoyu requires about one year—please refer to "Shoyu Production Process") and the calorie content, etc. She gave instructions to the effect that amino acids derived from breaking down the protein of soybeans with acid be used rather than brewed shoyu, and planned to curtail the allotment of soybeans to makers of brewed shoyu. A preference for certain flavors, she maintained, is an easily changed habit.

Shoyu cannot be made without soybeans. Japanese shoyu itself was in grave danger of being obliterated at that time.

The shoyu industry then, for its own benefit as well as for the benefit of the shoyu-loving populace as a whole, was forced into the position of discovering a faster shoyu brewing process that would not compare unfavorably with in point of amino acid yield, production time, calorie content, etc. and yet yield a product with a satisfying flavor. And subsequently persuading the lady at GHQ.

Japanese scientists came up with a perfected method in July, 1948. Miss Appleton was convinced and the allotment of soybeans for shoyu production was increased.

Now, shoyu is being used by Americans and is welcomed as a "new" flavor. In this sense, Americans themselves may be changing their taste preferences—the passage of time provides many ironies. I have no bitterness. But neither am I trying to laugh off this insignificant incident falling between Louis XIV and current American consumers. Rather, I wish to emphasize only that the value of shoyu is in its flavor and that people's taste-preferences are not easily changed things.

The thinking that "Shoyu's main constituent is amino acids and therefore a chemically produced amino acid solution should be satisfactory" may be compared to a theory that wine or whiskey's main constituent is ethyl alcohol (who can oppose this?) and therefore dissolving ethyl alcohol in water will have the desired results.

There is one important element that cannot be ignored in human food and especially in flavoring. And that is flavor.

Shoyu Production Process

Shoyu Production Process

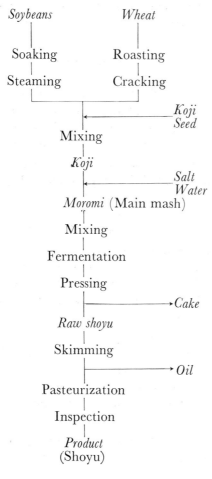

Soybeans   Wheat

Soaking   Roasting

Steaming   Cracking

Koji Seed

Mixing

Koji

Salt Water

Moromi (Main mash)

Mixing

Fermentation

Pressing

→ Cake

Raw shoyu

Skimming

→ Oil

Pasteurization

Inspection

Product (Shoyu)

Shoyu, simply stated, is obtained from the chemical break-down of soybean and wheat components in the presence of salt and by the operations of micro-organisms. Wheat components give shoyu its fragrance and coloring and soybean components give it its flavor and reddish hues. Salt, of course, gives it its salty taste.

The shoyu production process evolved over the centuries and by the beginning of the 19th century it had been standardized, providing us with approximately the same high quality we enjoy today.

Then, as Japan was exposed to modern science (at about the beginning of the 20th century) this unique seasoning and its manufacturing process came under investigation by scientists. Further, as chemical analysis techniques and mechanical technology were introduced, shoyu production developed into a modern industry at an amazing pace. These revolutionary developments were at least as earth-shaking to the Japanese as the beginnings of bio-chemistry were to the Europeans, when Louis Pasteur appeared and unlocked the secrets of wine composition, at the same time overturning the firmly entrenched theory of spontaneous generation. Both, in short, were times of great awakening.

More will be written about components later. In the meantime, let's examine the striking changes in equipment that were brought about in this process of modernization.

At present, large barrels for brewing have been replaced by stainless steel tanks; stirring formerly done by hand or foot has been automated; for the culture of micro-organisms, formerly dependent on "sixth sense," selected strains in isolation are utilized; and in the huge plant areas pipelines criss-cross in all directions, looking like something from a science fiction movie. Brightly shining modern facilities—conveyers, roasters, steamers, presses, sterilizers, bottling machines, fillers, can seamers, tanks—hum in the midst of a plant area almost empty of humans. The quietly functioning, gigantic plant brings together the essence of modern science and engineering in an impressive exhibition of technology.

At the center of all this—independent of human power in spite of the fact that they are 100% infused with human knowledge—are the fermentation tanks. No longer dependent upon human hands and feet, they are ignored for several months or sometimes a year except for an occasional stirring. Inside those tanks, however, micro-organisms are busy breaking down the soybean and wheat components and brewing that magnificent shoyu. This is the world of micro-organisms. About the only human work that can be done during this period is temperature control, occasional stirring and checking of the fermentation progress. It goes without saying that this fermentation process is the most important part of the entire shoyu brewing process.

Even though the equipment has been modernized, the scientific principles of shoyu production remain much the same. It may be said that the mystery of the birth of shoyu remains even after these several hundred years.

Let's look into the shoyu manufacturing process from the fermentation stage. Please refer to the block diagram while reading.

Raw Materials

Soybeans are often called "meat from the fields." They are rich in fat, and provide the well-known soybean oil that is used in cooking.

The special nutritional value of soybeans, however, is in their protein content. Among farm crops soybeans contain the greatest amount of protein. Further, the balance and type of amino acids comprising that protein is very similar to that of beef and pork. In Japan, where except for occasional sea food and poultry the national diet has long been semi-vegetarian, six types of processed soybean food, beginning with 'tofu' (the bean curd used in sukiyaki), and two types of soybean-based seasonings have become indispensable.

Recently, research is being undertaken in "synthetic meat" made from ex-oleated (fat-removed) soybeans with added flavor and consistency similar to domestic animal meat. We must say, however, that Japan's traditional soybean products have stolen the march on protein utilization.

Wandering away from the main point for a moment, it is thought that the vigor and longevity of monks living under the strict discipline of Zen temples without any fish or animal protein derivatives is due to their full utilization of soybeans and sesame seeds. Actually, some of the soybean products and cuisine utilizing those products mentioned earlier were developed by monks in Zen temples.

Shoyu contains almost all of the nutritious components of those superb soybeans. The protein changes into various types of amino acids but it may be stated that the nutritional value remains the same because protein follows an identical

course during the digestion process within our bodies. It may further be stated that we are merely advancing the digestion process when we consume shoyu. Of course, we can't consume enough shoyu to make the nutritional elements meet our daily needs but we may certainly use it as a seasoning with complete confidence that it is a natural, healthful product.

The soybeans used for shoyu are almost exclusively produced in the United States. Another main ingredint of shoyu—wheat—is also a product of the U.S. It may therefore be stated that shoyu is a product in which Japanese traditional technology has altered the structure of the American raw material. It may be appropriate that America is the largest consumer of shoyu outside of Japan.

The soybeans are carefully selected, washed and soaked in water for about three hours. These operations may be considered routine but later operations, and ultimately the final product itself, will be greatly affected by any foreign objects contained in the raw materials. These operations, therefore, require great care and prudence. (At present, it is known that the fat contained in soy beans has little effect on the flavor, and good quality exoleated soybeans are also utilized.)

Next the soybeans are steamed to make them soft, so that the useful microorganisms can be more easily propagated.

Wheat After careful selection, the wheat is roasted. The fragrance and coloring of shoyu is greatly affected by this roasting process. A fluidized roaster is used and the roasted wheat is left alone for one night and then cracked (one grain into 3 or 4 pieces). For this, a roller mill is used.

Salt is dissolved in water in preparation for mixing with other ingredients.

Koji Making

Koji may be defined as one type of mold culture. Koji molds (mainly *Aspergillus*) are grown on soybeans and grains for the production of sake, soybean paste ('miso') and shoyu. In the case of shoyu, the koji breaks down the protein and starch in soybeans and wheat with enzymes that it produces.

The "tane koji" (seed or inoculum for making koji) is mixed with the soybeans or wheat after the processing mentioned earlier; a suitable temperature (about 93°F) is maintained; the tane koji seedlings propagate and grow, covering the surface of the soybeans and wheat while the spawn work underneath. The soybean and wheat tissue become fragile; the protein is decomposed by the action of proteinase and becomes amino acids, while the starch is broken down by amylase and is turned into various sugars. The koji continues its work for three days and on the fourth, it is withdrawn.

24

Koji making

Moromi ageing

Formerly, in the making of koji according to the "cut and try" method, a small amount of koji was utilized as seed for making the next koji, but in 1904 as a result of technical research at Kikkoman, a good, pure culture was obtained from shoyu koji. Since that time, this pure strain has been used as "tane koji" to effect stabilization of the product.

Pressing

Fermentation and Brewing

Next, we'll go into the brewing process. The prepared koji is mixed with the separately prepared salt solution and put into the tanks for ageing. The syrupy product resulting from ageing is called "moromi" (mash). These states of koji and moromi are invariably passed through in the production of shoyu.

The brewing process can continue for about one year with occasional stirring and feeding of air (oxygen) under pressure. This type of fermentation is called "aerobic fermentation." Because brewing is on a large scale and is carried out for a long period—about one year—special buildings are necessary. These are the long brewing warehouses with white walls and tiled roofs, which have come to symbolize shoyu production.

Let's look into the chemical changes which occur during brewing. First, when salt is mixed in, the koji propagation weakens. Due to the action of the enzymes contained in the koji, amino acids and sugars increase. At the same time, yeast multiplies and the sugar content is broken down, changing to alcohols. Alcohol is one of the main constituents, giving body to the aroma of shoyu.

Also, bacteria such as lactobacilli propagate and assume dominance. The subsequently produced organic acids, beginning with lactic acid, become the chief components of flavor and the compounds formed from these organic acids and alcohols—esters—are the components of bouquet.

Meanwhile the soybeans and wheat lose their form and the 'moromi' mask becomes a reddish-brown liquid.

Pressing

At the completion of this long, patient brewing, the process is similar to that of other liquid food production processes. The syrupy 'moromi' is pressed and the oil is removed from the fluid thus obtained. This "raw shoyu" is then heated and pasteurized. With heat application, the no-longer-needed micro-organisms are eliminated and both color and fragrance improve. The bottling or canning process follows.

Shoyu Components

Shoyu may be called an orchestration of flavors. The various flavors intermingle to compose shoyu's unique taste.

The Components of Bouquet

The bouquet of shoyu is truly amazing. It has been the object of scientific research in Japan for these several decades. The dramatic changes in bouquet that occur during brewing and the very complexity of this bouquet found in the midst of their daily lives no doubt gave impetus to these scientists in their research. The components in the aroma of shoyu that have been isolated and identifed to date by these scientists are:

Alcohols—9 types
Aldehydes and Ketones—17 types
Acetals—2 types
Organic Acids—9 types
Esters—9 types
Sulphur compounds—2 types
(one is conjecture, the other an alcohol derivative)

There are more than 100 components in total.

Among these, there is one which closely resembles a component in the aroma of coffee. This is believed to be the reason for most Westerners liking the aroma of shoyu at first tasting. The familiar vanilla fragrance found in cakes, cookies and ice cream is also contained in the bouquet of shoyu. These are also components to be found in the bouquet of whiskey. And esters are the chemical compounds that compose the fragrances of fruits and flowers such as roses and hyacinths. Ketones are also components in the fragrance of fruits. And diacetal is a component found in the aroma of butter. Many of the components of the smoked flavor found in whiskey, ham and sausages are also to be found in shoyu.

Further, there are substances first isolated in shoyu and considered special characteristics of the shoyu bouquet. These include methionol (3-mercaptopropylalcohol), soyanal and shoyualdehyde. Methionol is one of the specific flavors of shoyu's special fragrance and is the fruition of early research by internationally famous biochemist Dr. Shiro Akabori. Due to the fact that methionol is a relatively simple chemical compound and due also to the inclination of the discoverer, it is not designated by the name 'shoyu' but I'm sure you realize that the other two are. ("Soy" is the English equivalent of "shoyu".)

Many compounds have been identified as flavor components of shoyu, but no "chief component" has been found. The reason is that such a component doesn't exist as a single substance. It is the whole which is greater than the sum of its parts. With all of these varied componds intermingled in the bouquet of shoyu, it isn't a question of finding one that stands out but, rather, shoyu is that which harmonizes this admixture of natural aromas.

The bouquet of shoyu doesn't exist in other things. It is one bouquet. But it is also an orchestration of the aromas of all foods.

Flavor Components

The components of taste are also numerous. As related earlier, the chemically organic components of shoyu are amino acids created from the breakdown of protein. Those products now widely used as "flavor enhancers," monosodium glutamate lysine, glycine, alanine, aspertic acid, etc.—are all present in large amounts in shoyu and, indeed, compose shoyu's deliciousness. (Please refer to "Shoyu and Health".)

Shoyu also contains ethyl alcohol. Of course, sine the wheat starch goes though the same course and changes as in alcohol fermentation. Alcoholic beverages such as wine, whiskey and vodka are widely used as flavorings in many parts of the world. In fact, they are the secrets to the success of good cooks. In addition to imparting a pleasing flavor to cuisine because of its flavor and fragrance components, alcohol also serves to heat uniformly, to aid in the permeation of flavor and to enhance all other flavors.

Shoyu has a pH of about 5 and contains about 2% lactic acid. Compared with acetic acid, the main component of vinegar, lactic acid, imparts a more refined, rounder acidity, much as those lactic acid foods made from milk (yogurt, etc.). In addition, there are more than ten other organic acids contained in shoyu. Among them is succinic acid, a component necessary for the special flavor of shellfish (clams, etc.).

Sugars are also contained in shoyu. Of course, the main one is glucose obtained from the break-down of starch, but there are more than ten additional types. Actually, one scientist was amazed, after extracting the salt from shoyu by a special method, at the resultant sweetness.

Salt (Sodium chloride) gives shoyu, of course, its salinity. The density is from 12 to 18%. The Japanese obtain 30% of their salt requirements from shoyu.

Nevertheless, the fact that shoyu is salty does not mean that it is merely used as a salt flavoring. It is essential in the production process. If the salt components are lessened, the lactobacilli and yeast will act differently to produce a product with quite different flavor. This density of salt is also necessary to protect shoyu, with its large concentrations of amino acids, from spoiling. There is no preservative other than salt in shoyu. And it is quite remarkable how long this flavoring can be maintained even after opening the container.

The Coloring of Shoyu

Good shoyu is translucent with a beautiful reddish-brown coloration. This is believed to be the result of the principle of Maillard's reaction on the amino acids and sugars (or other aldehydes) during the brewing and heating process. That is, the more the components in the basic flavor, the deeper the color will become. In other words, there is also the possibility that the flavor will be adversely affected by the flavor components changing into coloring elements, if the color is ridiculously deep.

Incidentally, the coloring process will continue if the shoyu is permitted to remain in contact with the oxygen in the air after opening. The flavor will be affected to some degree. Because this reaction may be controlled with low temperatures, it is good to keep the opened shoyu containers in the refrigerator.

Shoyu and Cooking

Shoyu is a seasoning that can be used with almost every dish in various ways, so it is often called the "all-purpose seasoning." It can also be used at the dining table but its true merits come to light when used with hot dishes. When you add shoyu while dishes are cooking, changes occur, changes that only shoyu can bring about. Through these changes the flavor of most dishes is considerably improved.

In the first place there is the "roasting aroma." When amino acids and carbohydrates are heated in the presence of very little water to over 320°F, aromas are set free. These fragrant smells are caused by the so-called Strecker degradation and other reactions, which occur when both amino acids and carbohydrates are present and react on each other. You have certainly noticed this effect when coffee, nuts or meat are being roasted. Shoyu itself contains considerable amounts of amino acids. When it is put on food or the food is allowed to soak in it before cooking, the amino acid reacts with the food and you get an excellent roasting aroma. That is why shoyu goes just perfectly with steak, teriyaki and other meat dishes.

In the second place shoyu can also be used with boiled food. The amino acids of the shoyu soak deep into the food and when you boil it new aromas are very often set free by reaction with the food content. This means that you do not simply add the shoyu flavor to sukiyaki and other dishes that are prepared with a sauce based on shoyu, but that you enhance the characteristic flavor of the food itself.

When there is a smell of tomato sauce coming from the kitchen you can tell that there is something being cooked with tomato sauce, but you do not know what it is. However, in the case of shoyu just a little sniff will be enough for any Japanese to tell you exactly what is being cooked.

According to the report of an American scientist a completely different chocolate brand is obtained when certain amino acids are added during the manufacturing process. So we can see that amino acids are important elements indeed in the taste and flavor of foods.

In the third place there is the multiplier effect of amino acids and nucleotides, which will be explained in detail in the chapter "Shoyu and Health." By interaction of these two flavor components, the feeling of "tastiness" is strongly enhanced. Meat contains nucleotides, and when you taste it together with the amino acids of shoyu its tastiness is many times increased.

Shoyu and Health
Japanese Cooking, a Healthy Diet

Shoyu is "digested soybean protein"

Shoyu is made from soybeans and wheat and in the manufacturing process 80–90% of their constituent proteins and starch is broken down into amino acids, sugars and so forth. When you eat soybeans and wheat they are broken down just the same way; however, roasted soybeans can only be digested to 60% and boiled soybeans to about 70%. So when you consume shoyu your protein intake percentage is much higher.

Taste and Digestion

However, shoyu is not "food" eaten for its nutritive value. A little shoyu gives taste to a dish, enhances its flavor—this is perhaps the only task shoyu has to fulfill.

Good shoyu stimulates the secretion of gastric juice, that is, it has the same beneficial effect as the caffeine in a cup of coffee.

Therefore it can be said that shoyu acts simultaneously both as an excellent appetizer and a digestive aid.

Tastiness Versus Fat (Japanese Cooking Versus Western Cooking)

The most important contribution that shoyu makes to a healthful diet is perhaps its "tastiness." "Tastiness" is a term that appears quite often in this book, and there might be people who are not very familiar with it. It is a particular taste which the vegetarian Japanese have cherished from olden times.

This brings up the subject of how many primary tastes we can actually distinguish. Since early times scientists and psychologists have concentrated their interest on this question. The question touches upon the fields of chemistry, neurophysiology, dietetics, food science, and biochemistry. For several thousand years various scientists of many countries have been suggesting different combinations of "primary tastes." These theories incidentally throw some interesting light on the eating habits and cultures of different nations. Some time ago a psychologist named Henning put forward a theory that the four "primary tastes" are "sweet, sour, salty and bitter." (Figure 1).

These four primary tastes of Henning's reflect, of course, the experience of people in America and Europe, and this is no doubt why his theory was widely accepted in these countries.

The Japanese, however, could not accept this theory, because for them there is still another important primary taste, "tastiness." It is not sweet, not sour, not salty, not bitter and can only be described as tasty. Take for instance dried bonito, dried *shiitake* (a kind of mushroom) or dried tangle. When you boil them in salt water, the original salty taste will become rounded and you get a new "tastiness." In 1908 a Japanese chemist extracted monosodium glutamate from dried tangle and proved that it was a constituent of "tastiness." Since then MSG (monosodium glutamate) has been marketed in Japan, and later in other countries including America. This "tastiness" is also present, although not as strongly, in various amino acids. Another "tastiness" can be found in the nucleotides (inosinic acid and guanilic acid). Therefore Japanese scientists added "tastiness" to Henning's four primary tastes and advocated the theory of five primary tastes.

Of course, this theory met with stiff resistance on the part of American and European scientists. One scientist even proved that a taste similar to monosodium glutamate can be obtained when the prime materials (sugar, tartaric acid, table salt, caffeine) of the four primary tastes are appropriately mixed.

Nowadays, however, "tastiness" has more and more come to be scientifically recognized as one of the primary tastes of man. This has been proved by neuro-physiologic experiments.

The well-known French gourmet *Brillat-Savarin* published his famous book "The physiology of Taste, or Meditation of Transcendant Gastronomy" in 1825. In this book he mentions "osmazôme" by which he means "the flavor components in meat which dissolve in cold water." According to Brillat-Savarin these components are obtained from adult animals having red or dark meat, and are different from the extract that does not dissolve in cold water. The chemical properties of this "osmazôme" somehow remind us of amino and inosinic acids. In this connection it may be added that the "extract that does not dissolve in cold water" probably is fat.

Figure 2 is a representation of our sense of taste when we give due recognition to "tastiness." Here we have put Henning's four basic tastes at the corners of a two-dimensional figure. This figure serves as the base for a pyramid with "tastiness" at the apex. With only Henning's four tastes, no matter how we combine and mix them, we get nothing more than a "flat" two-dimensional taste. The role of "tastiness" is precisely to give depth, a third dimension, or in other words "body," to taste. After all, our own bodies are three dimensional, you know!

At any rate the Japanese have always cherished this "tastiness." They have extracted it from various materials and have thought up ways to make their vegetarian diet tastier. The history of the Japanese cuisine can be described as a passionate devotion to "tastiness," a continuous quest for this precious seasoning. Rather than being just another seasoning, shoyu can be called one of the perfect seasonings that give dishes this characteristic tastiness.

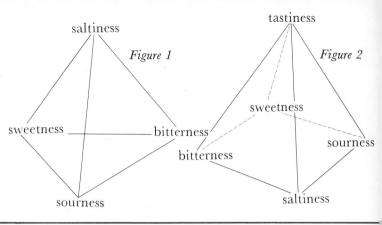

Figure 1. **Henning's idea of a 4 basic taste tetrahedron. The taste of any food can be expressed as a point located somewhere on the surface of this tetrahedron.**

Figure 2. **The 5 basic taste pyramid (according to the author's experience). The taste of any food can be expressed as a point located somewhere on one of the surfaces, on one of the borderlines on at one of the five apexes.**

The American and the European palates, however, seem yet to be awakened to this tastiness; at least there have been no efforts made in these countries to find a similar seasoning. What could be the reason for this?

Most Americans eat steak with salt and pepper and find it very tasty that way. Should there be any necessity to make it even more tasty? When I was at the Worcester Foundation for Experimental Biology near Boston I once explained "tastiness" to a graduate student. But when I had finished I was quite taken aback by his remark: "You may be quite right there, Dr. Otsuka, but as far as steak is concerned you just have to sprinkle a little salt on it and you get the greatest taste in the world."

You may say that this is just a matter of taste but the culture of a nation is also expressed in its taste. So I should like to treat this matter a bit more in detail.

As I have mentioned before, shoyu contains 18% salt, however, it does not seem to be that salty. This is because the "tastiness" substances (amino acids etc.) in shoyu make the sharp taste of salt milder and rounder. This is the main effect of "tastiness."

When we turn to Western cuisine we find that other agents are used to take the sharpness out of salt, namely oil and fat. In fact, we can say that the most important feature of European cuisine is that a lot of oils and fats are used. You may object that people cook differently in every European country, but in the final analysis it boils down to the fact that they only use different oils. American cuisine has adopted this European tradition and also uses comparatively large amounts of oil. And without being aware of it Americans get a high intake of fat with the beef and pork they eat. Americans eat almost three times more fat per day than Japanese do.

There is a simple explanation why the taste of salt is weakened and made rounder when oil or fat is present. This is caused by the effect of the emulsified oil or simply of oil which spreads like a film over the tongue and makes it less sensitive.

This may be called the most important difference between Japanese and Western cooking.

A Japanese scientist has said that from the standpoint of cooking the world can be divided into two hemispheres, one which employs oil and the other which does not. In the latter hemisphere people would rely on amino acids, etc. to take the pungency out of salt and make its taste rounder, and consequently in this part of the world "tastiness" would have been developed to a higher degree.

31

This theory explains neatly why a fat steak becomes tasty when you just sprinkle on some salt or why dressings with oil give taste to salads which do not contain any fat.

Oil versus shoyu (tastiness)—this is the difference between Western and Japanese cuisine which manifests itself extremely clearly in their contrasting tastes.

Among the conclusions which can be drawn there is a very important one. The intelligent reader will probably already know what I am driving at. Right! "Shoyu can replace oil and fats!"

It is almost self-evident that fat is the chief culprit in causing obesity. Let me quote the following passage from "Low-Fat Cookery" by Dr. Stead and Dr. Warren.

"Fat in the diet is of particular importance in the problem of obesity because an ounce of fat contains more than twice the calories present in an ounce of sugar or protein. Many doctors believe that the large fat intake in the average American diet plays an important role in hardening of the arteries and that persons of normal weight should derive less of their calories from fat.

One ounce of fat supplies more than twice as many calories as an equal amount of carbohydrate or protein. Therefore, when one wishes to reduce weight, limitation of fat intake is much more efficient than decreasing the intake of carbohydrate (sugar and starch) or protein.

If one decreases the daily intake of fat from the normal American level of some 100 grams, or often more, to 50 grams of fat or less, weight will be lost unless the total quantity of food eaten is increased. Low-fat cookery is the answer to weight control in those people who enjoy the pleasure of the table."

The necessity of a low-fat diet is laid down here, for the attainment of which the authors present many low-fat recipes using, for instance, lean beef and fat-removed chicken and fish, and recommend skimming soup by means of bread or lettuce leaves. The book was published in 1956 but the authors were apparently not aware of the existence of shoyu. At least the book does not contain any suggestions to make use of it. However, these low-fat recipes would definitely be much more delicious when prepared with shoyu.

One gram of fat contains about nine calories, whereas one gram of shoyu has only about 0.7, which can be considered negligible. Even if you use shoyu in the quantities necessary to obtain a satisfying taste, its caloric value is very low. And as a bonus you get a good aroma.

This is why shoyu is ideal for people who want to slim, for those who do not want to put on weight or have to watch their blood pressure. In short, shoyu is good for your health, for your beauty, and furthermore, it pleases your palate.

I have a good proof for this assertion. 100 million slim, active Japanese!

Among Japanese tourists or other people coming from Japan it is quite unusual to detect a stout person. On the other hand, most of the Japanese who have stayed one or two years in the States have put on weight by the time they return to Japan. They simply say it is because the "food is so good." In Japan, too, conditions have changed a little and obesity has become a problem to some extent. America is a rich country, and Americans certainly pay high prices for their food, but recently there has been much argument about whether it is really nutritous, or even suitable for a human diet. This matter certainly will have to be reexamined in the future. On the other hand, Japanese eating habits cannot be termed ideal either. However, for the time being let me end this argument by quoting again from the report of the missionaries who came to Japan in the 15th century.

". . . but even with this simple food the people here are very healthy, and we were surprised by the great number of old people."

Conclusion
Shoyu Is for All Mankind

In San Fransisco there is a restaurant which is said to serve "Kikkoman Steak" as one of its specialties. There are already quite a few restaurants where shoyu is used for delicious dishes. And the day might not be too far away when all American restaurants will employ shoyu as a secret seasoning which would enable them to serve their customers delicious and still inconspicuously seasoned dishes just like the chef of Louis XIV.

It should be no surprise that shoyu suits the palate of Americans and Europeans. It is said that among instant soups made by a famous European company you find a product that shows a striking similarity to Japanese shoyu.

It is a special feature of shoyu that it can be mixed with other ingredients to make a new sauce. Thunberg, whom I mentioned before, said that shoyu can be mixed with any sauce you can think of. Barbecue sauce, cutlet sauce, teriyaki sauce and Japanese Worchester sauce—they are all made with a shoyu base. Without being aware of it you might eat shoyu-seasoned foods quite often.

An Italian lady who is proud of her cooking once told me after having been in Japan two years: "Look, I've invented a new sauce." And then she started mixing mayonnaise and shoyu and made me try it. Because it is rather difficult to get shoyu in Italy, she said, she would take a lot of shoyu back with her.

At first I was surprised that the people who can claim the honor of having invented the tomato sauce, which seems to have conquered the whole world, could get so excited about shoyu. But then I thought it was only natural because the Latin people have always eagerly sought "tastiness." Very often we do not appreciate things we are too familiar with. This incident convinced me that in the future shoyu would spread all over the world and that the day is not too far away when it will be used as a seasoning in every country. It only makes me wonder why shoyu was not internationalized much earlier.

Here is shoyu. We give it to you. It is yours. The Japanese have invented various dishes which become more delicious when seasoned with shoyu. Now you can create new recipes, season your dishes with shoyu and make them more delicious. It is all up to your creativeness.

RECIPES WITH BREWED SOY SAUCE

From the Kikkoman Cooking Center and *Kikkoman Cook Book*

Appetizers

MENEHUNE CHICKEN

  24 chicken wings
   1 cup **KIKKOMAN** Soy Sauce
 3/4 cup finely chopped green onions and tops
 1/3 cup sugar
   1 tablespoon salad oil
   1 clove garlic, crushed
1-1/2 teaspoons ground ginger (or 1 tablespoon grated fresh ginger root)

Disjoint chicken wings; discard tips. Blend soy sauce, green onions, sugar, oil, garlic and ginger in large bowl. Add chicken pieces and marinate 30 minutes. Remove chicken; reserve marinade. Place chicken in single layer in shallow baking pan. Bake, uncovered, in 350° oven 15 minutes. Turn pieces, baste with marinade, and bake 15 minutes longer.   Makes about 4 dozen appetizers.

CHICKEN KABOBS (Yakitori)

2-1/2 to 3 pounds chicken breasts
   1 pound chicken livers
   1 bunch green onions
   1 cup **KIKKOMAN** Soy Sauce
1/4 cup sugar
  1 tablespoon salad oil
  2 cloves garlic, crushed
3/4 teaspoon ground ginger

Remove skins and bones from chicken breasts, keeping meat in one piece; cut into 1-inch squares. Cut livers into 1-inch pieces and onions into 1-inch lengths. Thread bamboo skewers each with a chicken piece, a green onion piece (spear through side) and a chicken liver piece. Blend together soy sauce, sugar, oil, garlic and ginger. Place kabobs in large shallow baking pan; pour sauce over. Brush each kabob thoroughly with sauce. Marinate kabobs about 1 hour and remove; reserve marinade. Broil kabobs 5 inches below preheated broiler 3 minutes on each side, brushing with marinade after turning. Serve immediately. Makes about 4 dozen kabobs.

CHINESE BARBECUED PORK (Char Siu)

        1/2 cup KIKKOMAN Soy Sauce
        1/3 cup honey
        1/4 cup sherry
          1 teaspoon red food coloring
        1/4 teaspoon ground ginger (or 1 teaspoon grated fresh ginger
             root)
        1/4 teaspoon garlic powder
          2 pounds boneless pork loin roast
            Mustard-Soy Sauce
        1/3 cup sesame seed, toasted

Blend together soy sauce, honey, sherry, food coloring, garlic and ginger in large
mixing bowl. Unroll pork roast; cut lengthwise into 3 strips. Add to soy sauce
marinade; turn over several times to coat thoroughly. Cover bowl and refrigerate
12 to 24 hours; turn over occasionally. Remove pork from sauce; lay on rack
placed over pan of water. Insert meat thermometer in thickest part of one strip.
Roast in 325° oven 30 minutes. Turn pork over, roast 30 minutes longer, or until
meat thermometer reads 185°. Cool slightly before slicing; cut each pork strip into
thin slices. Serve with Mustard-Soy Sauce and sesame seed.
Mustard-Soy Sauce:
   Blend 2 tablespoons dry mustard with water to make a smooth paste. Thin with
   Kikkoman Soy Sauce to dipping consistency. Makes about 4 dozen appetizers.

MUSHROOM HORS D'OEUVRES

        1/3 cup rice wine vinegar
          1 tablespoon sugar
          2 teaspoons KIKKOMAN Soy Sauce
            Dash MSG
          1 can (4 oz.) whole mushrooms, drained
            Toasted sesame seed, if desired

Thoroughly combine vinegar, sugar, soy sauce and MSG. Pour over mushrooms
and sprinkle with sesame seed. Marinate 30 to 60 minutes. Remove from sauce and
serve as appetizers.
OR: pour sauce over drained whole water chestnuts; marinate several hours or
   overnight in refrigerator.

CALIFORNIA BEEF JERKY

    1 flank steak (1-1/2 to 2 pounds)
1/2 cup KIKKOMAN Soy Sauce
1/4 teaspoon garlic salt
1/4 teaspoon lemon and pepper seasoning

Trim all visible fat from steak. Cut lengthwise with grain into long thin strips, no more than 1/4-inch thick. Combine soy sauce with garlic salt and lemon and pepper seasoning. Pour over beef strips and toss to coat well. Place wire rack on large baking sheet. Arrange strips on rack to touch, being careful not to overlap. Bake in 150° to 175° oven overnight, 10 to 12 hours, or until thoroughly dry. Store at room temperature in air tight container.

CURRY DIP

    1 large package (8 oz.) cream cheese, softened
    6 tablespoons water
    1 tablespoon KIKKOMAN Soy Sauce
    1 teaspoon curry powder

Blend together cream cheese, water, soy sauce and curry powder until smooth. Serve as dip for fresh fruits and/or vegetables. Makes about 1 cup.

SESAME DIP

    2 tablespoons sesame seed, toasted
    1 large package (8 oz.) cream cheese, softened
    6 tablespoons water
    1 tablespoon KIKKOMAN Soy Sauce
  1/4 teaspoon hot pepper sauce

Crush sesame seed in blender at high speed; add cream cheese, water, soy sauce and hot pepper sauce; blend well. Serve as dip for fresh fruits and/or vegetables. Makes about 1 cup.

WESTERN NUTS AND EASTERN BOLTS

    2 cups bite-size shredded rice biscuits
    2 cups bite-size shredded corn
      or wheat biscuits
    2 cups dry-roasted salted peanuts
  1/2 cup melted butter or margarine
  1/4 cup KIKKOMAN Teriyaki Sauce
  1/2 teaspoon garlic powder
  1/4 teaspoon celery salt
    1 cup pretzel sticks

Gently toss together rice biscuits, corn biscuits and peanuts in large baking pan. Combine butter, teriyaki sauce, garlic and celery salt; pour over peanut mixture. Bake in 250° oven 15 minutes; stir gently with wooden spoon. Return to oven and bake 15 minutes longer. Cool thoroughly. Add pretzels and toss to combine. Makes about 8 cups.

Salads and Salad Dressing

ORIENTAL CUCUMBER SALAD (Sunomono)

    2 medium-size cucumbers, peeled and seeded
    2 teaspoons salt
  1/3 cup rice wine vinegar
    1 tablespoon sugar
    2 teaspoons KIKKOMAN Soy Sauce
  1/4 teaspoon grated fresh ginger root (or 1/8 teaspoon ground
      ginger)

Cut cucumbers into thin slices; place in bowl and sprinkle with salt. Let stand at room temperature 1 to 2 hours. Drain and squeeze out excess liquid. Combine vinegar, sugar, soy sauce and ginger in serving bowl; add cucumbers and mix well. Chill thoroughly before serving. Makes 4 servings.

CELERY VICTOR

2 or 3 small celery hearts	1/4 cup rice wine vinegar
1 medium-size onion, sliced	1 clove garlic, crushed
2-1/2 cups water	1/2 teaspoon sugar
1/4 cup KIKKOMAN Soy Sauce	1/2 teaspoon salt
1/2 cup salad oil	1/2 teaspoon dill weed, crushed

Wash celery hearts thoroughly; trim root ends and remove all but smallest leaves. Place onion and celery hearts in shallow saucepan or frying pan with cover. Add water and soy sauce. Cover pan; bring sauce to boil, reduce heat and simmer about 15 minutes or until celery is tender. Remove from heat and cool celery in sauce. Meanwhile, blend together oil, vinegar, garlic, sugar, salt and dill weed. Remove hearts from sauce, cut in half lengthwise and place in shallow dish. Pour vinegar dressing over celery. Cover and chill for several hours. To serve, drain off most of dressing and place celery on shredded iceberg lettuce. Makes 4 to 6 servings.

SALAD "NICE" STYLE

    3 **medium potatoes, cooked in jackets and peeled**
    1 **tablespoon KIKKOMAN Soy Sauce**
    1 **small head iceberg lettuce, torn into bite-size pieces**
    1 **stalk celery, thinly sliced**
    1 **medium cucumber, thinly sliced**
    1 **green pepper, cut into rings**
    1 **small onion, thinly sliced and separated into rings**
    1 **tomato, cut into wedges**
    1 **hard-cooked egg, cut into wedges**
       Anchovies and sliced olives, if desired
       Salad dressing

Cut potatoes into slices; cut each slice into quarters. Sprinkle soy sauce evenly over potatoes. In large salad bowl, gently toss together lettuce, potatoes, celery, cucumber, green pepper and onion. Arrange tomato and egg attractively on vegetables and garnish with anchovies and olives. Serve with salad dressing.

Salad Dressing:
  - **6 tablespoons salad oil**
  - **3 tablespoons rice wine vinegar**
  - **1 tablespoon KIKKOMAN Soy Sauce**
  - **1 teaspoon minced parsley**
  - **Dash pepper**

Combine all ingredients. Makes 4 to 6 servings.

VINAIGRETTE SALAD DRESSING

  - **1 cup salad oil**
  - **1/3 cup vinegar**
  - **1 tablespoon KIKKOMAN Soy Sauce**
  - **1 tablespoon grated Parmesan cheese**
  - **1 tablespoon finely chopped green pepper**
  - **1 tablespoon finely chopped onion**
  - **1 tablespoon finely chopped pimiento**

Combine all ingredients and allow to stand at least 1 hour. Shake thoroughly before serving. Makes 1–1/2 cups.

Beef

BEEF SUKIYAKI

1-1/2 pounds boneless tender beef steak, sliced as thin as possible
  4 stalks celery, sliced diagonally into 1/2-inch pieces
  2 medium onions, thinly sliced
  1 bunch green onions and tops, cut into 2-inch lengths
1/2 pound fresh spinach leaves, blanched
  1 can (4 oz.) sliced mushrooms, drained
  1 can (8-1/2 oz.) sliced bamboo shoots, drained (if available)
  1 cup beef broth
1/2 cup KIKKOMAN Soy Sauce
1/4 cup water
  2 tablespoons sugar
  1 cup beef suet

Arrange beef and vegetables attractively on large platters. Combine broth, soy sauce, water and sugar; set aside. Turn electric skillet setting to 300°. Melt pieces of suet in skillet, stirring until pan is well coated. Remove browned suet. Place about 1/3 of the meat in skillet and pour 2/3 of the sauce over meat. Add 2/3 of each vegetables to skillet, keeping meat and vegetables in individual heaps. Turn ingredients gently while cooking, 5 to 6 minutes. Add another 1/3 of the meat and cook an additional 1 to 2 minutes. Serve cooked meat and vegetables immediately in individual bowls or plates. Replenish skillet with remaining ingredients and sauce, following cooking procedure. Makes about 4 servings.

BEEF TATSUTA STYLE

  1 pound boneless tender beef steak
1/4 cup KIKKOMAN Soy Sauce
  2 tablespoons sugar
1/4 cup flour (about)
   Vegetable oil for frying

Cut beef into 1-inch pieces. Blend together soy sauce and sugar. Dip pieces of beef first into soy sauce mixture, then coat with flour. Fry in deep hot fat (350°F.) until golden brown. Drain thoroughly on absorbent paper and serve on a napkin-lined plate. Makes 3 to 4 servings.

Sukiyaki— A "Japanese" Dish Coming Home to the West

by Shigeru Otsuka

A number of years ago there was a Japanese song that was quite a hit in America. There are quite a few people who will probably remember the "Sukiyaki Song." Actually, the original Japanese lyrics go, "Let's walk with our heads up high, so that the tears won't fall down . . . " In short, it was a rather sentimental song, and I have no idea what the connection with sukiyaki might be.

At that time I was working at a certain institute near Boston, and one morning, out of the blue, I was greeted by a man with "Good morning, Sukiyaki!", a greeting which more than somewhat bewildered me.

At any rate, sukiyaki now seems to represent Japan, or at least Japanese food, in the minds of many Americans.

In LIFE's "Picture Cook Book" there is the following passage under the heading "Flaming Food."

"One of the most festive ways to entertain formally is to cook, or finish cooking, the food right on the table, before the guests' eyes. It is also one of the most practical."

The book then shows photographs of international flaming foods: Swiss fondue, crepes Suzette, Mexican corn casserole and so forth. Among these, photos of sukiyaki ingredients and sukiyaki cooking style come in the first place.

And indeed, sukiyaki is very suitable for Americans who like to eat meat and to entertain at home, just as it is a delightful and practical dish for the Japanese.

Sukiyaki is one of the few Japanese dishes that Western people usually like from the start. This popularity of sukiyaki is probably due to two factors. The first is that it is the only Japanese dish that cannot be cooked without meat. The second and more important is that the meat, together with shoyu and sugar, create a complex and at the same time delicate taste that is not to be found in other meat dishes.

In Japan, common people did not eat meat for about 1200 years, since it had been forbidden by Imperial order in the first flush of religious fervor when Buddhism entered and spread through Japan. Beef, mutton, horsemeat, in fact the meat of all four-legged animals, was completely eliminated from the diet of the common people. Therefore in the late 19th century when the people, with considerable trepidation, started to eat beef, they were warned that they would develop tumors, that their hair would fall out, and other equally dire consequences would befall them. They were even told that what they were doing was an affront to their ancestors, that no good could come from such disrespectful behavior.

However, the people little by little came to eat beef, but not nearly as much as the government and the early intellectuals who were infatuated with Western culture and customs had hoped. Beef dishes like steak, roastbeef or stew, all quite common in the United States and Europe, have never gained wide popularity in Japan. Instead the Japanese began their beef-eating by slicing the meat thin, as they sliced fish for sashimi, and cooking it together with shoyu and vegetables. Which is to say they began their beef-eating with sukiyaki, and to this day sukiyaki is the most common way of preparing beef in Japan.

So we can say that beef has joined the family of traditional Japanese dishes that are prepared before your eyes. As a matter of fact, only a few ingenious ideas were necessary to adapt it to the Japanese way of cooking, and it did not take long until sukiyaki was cooked in its present style.

In the cooking of sukiyaki, shoyu has quite a dramatic effect. The shoyu flavor blends together with and brings out the flavor of the meat itself to create a completely new taste, a taste that people who like beef simply cannot help loving. Shoyu is the secret of this delicious taste, and knowing this, former American servicemen who had come to appreciate this taste in Japan spread its reputation to the States when they started to use shoyu with their steak.

Shoyu goes just perfectly with meat. Or I should say, rather than merely "going with" meat (which any mere sauce will do), shoyu brings forth the flavor of the meat itself. This was first proved to Western people, and in a very convincing way, by sukiyaki.

So as far as the material is concerned, sukiyaki is a Western dish. But the preparation and, most important, the seasoning, is Japanese.

Now, after an absence of nearly a hundred years, sukiyaki is " coming home" to the West. It has of course changed, so much that old friends and relatives can hardly recognize it. But it has become better because of its long stay abroad, it has picked up quite a few new things to show the folks back home. We wish you all a joyous reunion!

SHABU-SHABU

1-1/2 **pounds boneless beef sirloin or tenderloin, sliced as thinly as possible**
  1/2 **head Chinese cabbage, cut in 2-inch lengths**
    1 **cake tofu (soybean curd), cut in 1-inch cubes**
    8 **medium-sized fresh mushrooms, sliced**
    1 **bunch green onions, sliced in 2-inch lengths**
    1 **can (8-3/4 oz.) shirataki (yam noodles), drained**
    6 **cups water**
    1 **piece (4-inch square) kombu (dried kelp)**
      Dipping sauces

Arrange beef and vegetables attractively on large platter. Measure water into electric wok or large deep saucepan. Add kombu and bring to boil. Reduce heat to keep broth simmering. Place part of beef in broth and simmer for 2 to 3 seconds; add several pieces of each vegetable, keeping them separate. Simmer only until vegetables are tender. Remove beef and vegetables with chopsticks and

45

serve on individual plates. To eat, dip meat and vegetables into dipping sauces. When all the food is cooked, remove kombu and serve broth as soup. Makes 4 to 6 servings.

Dipping Sauce #1:

> **1/2 cup sesame seed, toasted**
> **1/2 cup rice wine vinegar·**
> **1/4 cup KIKKOMAN Soy Sauce**
> **1 tablespoon sugar**

Grind sesame seed on high speed in blender, add remaining ingredients and mix thoroughly. Pour into 4 to 6 small bowls.

Dipping Sauce #2:

> **1/2 cup chunk-style peanut butter**
> **2 tablespoons KIKKOMAN Soy Sauce**
> **1 teaspoon sugar**
> **1 teaspoon grated fresh ginger root**
> **1/2 cut water**

Thoroughly combine peanut butter, soy sauce, sugar and ginger. Add water and blend until smooth. Pour into 4 to 6 small bowls.

SHOYU-PICKLED BEEF

> **1/2 cup KIKKOMAN Soy Sauce**
> **1/2 cup mirin (sweet rice wine) or sherry**
> **2 cloves garlic, crushed**
> **1 pound boneless steak, thinly sliced**

Combine soy sauce, mirin and garlic. Arrange part of the beef slices in a single layer in shallow pan. Pour part of soy sauce mixture over beef. Repeat procedure with remaining beef and sauce. Marinate in refrigerator 12 to 24 hours. Remove from marinade and broil or grill to desired degree of doneness. Makes 2 to 4 servings.

FLANK STEAK

    1-1/2 **pounds flank steak**
      1/2 **cup KIKKOMAN Teriyaki Sauce**
        1 **tablespoon salad oil**
        1 **teaspoon lemon juice**

Remove fat from steak; score both sides in diamond pattern. Measure teriyaki sauce, oil and lemon juice into plastic bag. Add steak and coat thoroughly; seal with wire tie. Refrigerate 1 hour or more, keeping steak as flat as possible. Turn occasionally. Remove meat; reserve marinade. Broil meat 3 inches below pre-heated broiler 3 to 5 minutes on each side, brushing with marinade after turning. (On outdoor grill, broil steak 6 to 8 minutes on each side.) To serve, slice across grain in very thin slices. Makes 4 to 6 servings.

SWISS STEAK TERIYAKI

        2 **tablespoons flour**
  1-1/4 **to 1-1/2 pounds boneless beef round steak, 1/2-inch thick**
        1 **tablespoon shortening or oil**
        1 **medium onion, chopped**
        1 **cup water**
      1/2 **cup KIKKOMAN Teriyaki Sauce**
      1/4 **cup tomato catsup**

Pound flour thoroughly into steak. Cut meat into serving portions. Heat shortening or oil in large frying pan with cover. Add meat and brown over medium heat. Meanwhile, combine onion, water, teriyaki sauce and catsup; pour over meat. Bring mixture to boil; cover pan. Reduce heat and simmer 45 minutes to 1 hour, or until tender, turning meat over occasionally. Makes 4 to 6 servings.

LEMONY BEEF KABOBS

        1 **cup vinegar**
        2 **tablespoons olive oil**
        2 **tablespoons KIKKOMAN Soy Sauce**
        2 **teaspoons instant minced onion**
        1 **teaspoon tarragon leaves**
      1/2 **teaspoon black pepper**
      1/8 **teaspoon garlic powder**
        2 **pounds sirloin steak, 1 inch thick**

12 small whole bay leaves (or large leaves cut into 1-inch squares)

Combine vinegar, oil, soy sauce, onion, tarragon, pepper and garlic in saucepan. Bring to boil; remove from heat and cool thoroughly. Cut steak into pieces about 1 inch square; stir into sauce and marinate 1 hour. Remove ends from lemon and cut crosswise into 4 slices. Cut each slice into 3 wedge-shaped pieces. Thread skewers with a beef cube, a lemon wedge, a beef cube, a bay leaf and end with a beef cube. Broil 5 inches below preheated oven broiler or grill over charcoal to desired degree of doneness. Turn and brush often with marinade during cooking. Makes 4 servings.

KAUAI BEEF KABOBS

2 pounds boneless tender beef steaks, 3/4 inch thick
3/4 cup KIKKOMAN Teriyaki Sauce
1 can (1 lb. 4 oz.) pineapple chunks, drained
Cherry tomatoes

Cut steaks into 1-1/2-inch squares. Pour teriyaki sauce over beef and marinate about 30 minutes. Remove meat and reserve marinade. Thread skewers alternately with beef cubes, pineapple and tomatoes, beginning and ending with beef cubes. Brush kabobs thoroughly with reserved marinade. Broil to desired degree of doneness. Makes 4 to 6 servings.

MUSHROOM BURGERS

1 pound ground beef chuck
1 can (2 oz.) mushroom stems and pieces, drained and chopped
1/2 cup chopped onion
4 tablespoons KIKKOMAN Soy Sauce

Combine beef, mushrooms, onion and 2 tablespoons soy sauce until well blended. Shape into 4 patties. Heat frying pan until sizzling hot. Add patties and cook over medium heat 5 minutes, turn over and cook 4 to 6 minutes longer, or to desired degree of doneness. Remove patties from pan and stir in remaining 2 tablespoons soy sauce. Bring to rapid boil. Add patties, remove pan from heat and turn patties to coat both sides with soy sauce. Makes 4 servings.

SLOPPY JOES

    1 **can (16 oz.) tomatoes**
    1 **pound lean ground beef**
    1 **medium onion, chopped**
    5 **tablespoons KIKKOMAN Soy Sauce**
    1 **tablespoon prepared mustard**
    6 **hamburger and/or hot dog buns, split**

Drain tomatoes in collander or strainer. Break tomatoes, if whole, into smaller pieces (reserve drained liquid for another use). Brown beef with onion in large frying pan. Stir in tomatoes, soy sauce, mustard and pepper. Bring to boil, reduce heat and simmer, uncovered, 15 to 20 minutes, or until liquid is absorbed. Stir mixture occasionally. Spoon over bottom halves of buns, top with remaining halves. Makes 6 sandwiches.

MADHATTER MEATBALLS

      1 **pound ground beef**
      1 **small onion, finely chopped**
    1/4 **cup uncooked long-grain rice**
      1 **egg**
      2 **slices bread, torn in pieces**
      5 **tablespoons KIKKOMAN Soy Sauce**
      1 **can (10-3/4 oz.) condensed tomato soup**
      1 **cup water**

Blend beef, onion, rice, egg, bread and 1/4 cup soy sauce. Shape into 20 meatballs. In large frying pan with cover, blend tomato soup, water and 1 tablespoon soy sauce. Arrange meatballs, side by side, in soup mixture. Cover and simmer 1 hour, or until rice is cooked. Makes 4 servings.

50

TERIYAKI MEAT LOAF

    1-1/2 pounds ground beef
        1 large onion, chopped
     1/3 cup KIKKOMAN Teriyaki Sauce
        1 egg
        2 slices bread, torn in small pieces
     1/2 cup shredded sharp Cheddar cheese

Combine beef, onion, teriyaki sauce, egg and bread. Pat half of meat mixture onto bottom and sides of ungreased 8–1/2 ×4–1/2 ×2–1/2/inch loaf pan, forming a shell 1 inch thick. Sprinkle cheese evenly into meat shell; top with remaining meat. Bake in 350° oven 1 hour.

For Stuffed Meat Patties:

    Shape half of meat mixture for meat loaf into 6 patties and top with cheese, leaving a 1/2-inch margin around edges. Shape remaining meat mixture into 6 patties, place over cheese and seal edges firmly. Broil 5 inches below preheated broiler 5 minutes. Turn; broil 4 to 6 minutes longer, or to desired degree of doneness. Makes 4 to 6 servings.

BARBECUED SHORT RIBS

      5 pounds lean short ribs 3 to 4 inches long
    2/3 cup KIKKOMAN Teriyaki Sauce
    1/4 cup orange marmalade
      1 teaspoon garlic salt
    1/2 teaspoon lemon and pepper seasoning

Place short ribs in large bowl. Combine remaining ingredients; pour over ribs. Cover and refrigerate 8 to 10 hours or overnight, turning occasionally. Remove from marinade and drain thoroughly. Barbecue slowly on grill 7 to 8 inches from coals, 1–1/2 to 2 hours, or until meat begins to leave bone, turning frequently. Brush with marinade during last 20 minutes of cooking time. Makes 4 to 6 servings.

Chicken and Egg

CRISPY OVEN-FRIED CHICKEN

    2-1/2 to 3 pounds broiler-fryer chicken,
        cut up
    1/2 cup KIKKOMAN Soy Sauce
    1 cup corn flake crumbs

Wash chicken pieces and dry thoroughly. Beat egg in shallow dish or pan; stir in soy sauce until well blended. Dip chicken pieces in egg mixture and coat with corn flake crumbs. Place in single layer in greased or foil-lined shallow baking pan. Bake in 350° oven about 1 hour, or until chicken is tender. Serve with additional soy sauce. Makes 6 servings.

CHICKEN IN A BASKET

    2-1/2 to 3 pounds broiler-fryer chicken, cut up
    1/2 cup KIKKOMAN Soy Sauce
    1/2 cup flour (about)
    1/4 cup salad oil

Marinate chicken pieces in soy sauce about 15 minutes. Remove from sauce and coat thoroughly with flour. Place on cake rack or in wire basket and let dry, about 15 minutes. Heat oil in frying pan with cover. Brown chicken slowly on one side until light golden brown, 15 to 20 minutes. Turn chicken pieces over; add 1 teaspoon water. Cover pan and simmer chicken 20 minutes. Remove cover and cook an additional 10 minutes. Makes 4 servings.

BARBECUED CHICKEN FILLED KOREAN STYLE

    1/3 cup KIKKOMAN Soy Sauce
    3 tablespoons minced green onion
    1 tablespoon grated fresh ginger root
    1 teaspoon sesame seed, toasted
  1-1/2 teaspoons sesame seed oil (unrefined)
    1 clove garlic, finely chopped
    1/4 teaspoon cayenne pepper
    2 pounds chicken thighs, boned
    3 tablespoons salad oil

Thoroughly blend together soy sauce, green onion, ginger, sesame seed, sesame seed oil, garlic and cayenne. Cut chicken into bite-size pieces and add to sauce. Marinate about 30 minutes, stirring occasionally. Remove from marinade and drain. Heat oil in frying pan; add chicken, skin side down, and brown slowly over low heat. Turn chicken pieces over, and cook until tender. Makes 4 servings.

CHICKEN-CASHEW NUT SAUTE

  2 **whole chicken breasts, boned**
  1 **teaspoon sake (Japanese cooking wine) or dry white wine**
  1 **teaspoon grated fresh ginger root**
  1 **tablespoon cornstarch**
  1 **cup cashews or peanuts**
  3 **tablespoons salad oil**
  2 **tablespoons KIKKOMAN Soy Sauce**
  1 **tablespoon sake**
  1 **teaspoon sugar**
 1/2 **teaspoon cornstarch**
  1 **tablespoon water**

Remove and discard skin from chicken; cut meat into 1/2-inch cubes. Sprinkle 1 teaspoon sake and ginger over chicken and coat with 1 tablespoon cornstarch. Saute nuts in 1 tablespoon oil until golden brown over low heat. Remove from pan and set aside. Heat remaining oil, add chicken and stir-fry about 5 minutes, or until chicken is cooked. Season with soy sauce, 1 tablespoon sake and sugar. Dissolve cornstarch in water; stir into chicken mixture and cook until sauce thickens. Remove from heat and stir in nuts. Makes 3 to 4 servings.

GOURMET CHICKEN

>   2 tablespoons butter or margarine
>   2-1/2 to 3 pounds broiler-fryer chicken, cut up
>   1/2 cup KIKKOMAN Teriyaki Sauce
>   1/2 cup water
>   3 tablespoons frozen orange juice concentrate, thawed
>   1 tablespoon cornstarch

Melt butter in large frying pan with cover; add chicken pieces and brown thoroughly. Stir in teriyaki sauce, 1/4 cup water and orange juice. Bring mixture to boil; cover pan. Reduce heat and simmer 45 to 50 minutes, or until chicken is tender, turning pieces over occasionally. Remove chicken to platter. Combine cornstarch with remaining 1/4 cup water; stir into sauce in pan and bring to boil, stirring 1 minute. Spoon sauce over chicken or serve with chicken. Makes 4 servings.

CHICKEN CONFETTI

>   1 tablespoon butter or margarine
>   2-1/2 to 3 pounds broiler-fryer chicken, cut up
>   1 can (10-1/2 oz.) condensed cream of mushroom soup
>   2/3 cup water
>   2 tablespoons KIKKOMAN Soy Sauce
>   1 package (10 oz.) frozen mixed vegetables
>   3 tablespoons flour
>   1/4 cup cold water

Melt butter in large frying pan with cover. Add chicken; brown over medium heat. Remove chicken. In same frying pan, blend soup, 2/3 cup water and soy sauce; bring to boil. Add vegetables and separate with fork. Arrange chicken in sauce. Cover, reduce heat and simmer 45 minutes, or until chicken is tender, turning pieces occasionally. Blend flour and 1/4 cup water; stir into chicken mixture and cook until sauce thickens. Makes 4 servings.

CHICKEN VENETIAN

>   2-1/2 to 3 pounds broiler-fryer chicken, cut up
>   1/4 cup KIKKOMAN Soy Sauce
>   2 tablespoons lemon juice   1 clove garlic, crushed
>   1 tablespoon salad oil   1/4 teaspoon oregano, crumbled

Line bottom of shallow baking pan with aluminum foil. Arrange chicken pieces, side by side, on foil. Measure soy sauce, lemon juice, oil, garlic and oregano into small jar with cover. Cover jar and shake until sauce is well blended; pour over chicken. Turn pieces to coat thoroughly. Cover pan with another piece of aluminum foil, being careful to seal edges. Bake in 375° oven 45 minutes. Remove top foil, turn pieces over, and baste with sauce. Continue baking 15 minutes longer. Makes 4 servings.

"COME AGAIN" CHICKEN

2-1/2 to 3 pounds broiler-fryer chicken, cut up
3 tablespoons butter or margarine
1/2 cup chopped celery
1/2 cup chopped onion
1/2 cup KIKKOMAN Teriyaki Sauce
1/4 cup catsup

Brown chicken pieces slowly in butter or margarine. Sprinkle celery and onion evenly over chicken. Combine teriyaki sauce and catsup; pour over chicken and vegetables. Cover and simmer about 30 minutes, or until chicken is tender. Makes 4 servings.

SAUCE AND BAKE CHICKEN

    2-1/2 to 3 pounds broiler-fryer chicken, cut up
    1/2 cup KIKKOMAN Teriyaki Sauce
    1/4 cup water
    2 tablespoons chopped green onions and tops

Place 18 ×24-inch piece of heavy-duty aluminum foil in shallow baking pan. Arrange chicken pieces side by side on foil. Combine teriyaki sauce, water and green onions; pour over chicken. Turn chicken in sauce to coat thoroughly. Fold foil over chicken; seal securely. Bake in 400° oven 45 minutes. Carefully unfold foil, turn chicken over and baste with sauce. Leaving foil open, bake 15 minutes longer, or until chicken is tender, yet moist. Makes 4 servings.

SIMPLE SKILLET CHICKEN TERIYAKI

1/3 cup **KIKKOMAN** Soy Sauce
1/4 cup water
  2 tablespoons sugar
  1 clove garlic, crushed
1/4 teaspoon ground ginger
  1 tablespoon salad oil
  1 broiler-fryer chicken, cut up
    (2-1/2 to 3 pounds)

Thoroughly blend together soy sauce, water, sugar, garlic and ginger. Heat oil in large frying pan with cover. Add chicken and brown over medium heat until pieces are golden brown, about 15 minutes. Remove chicken; drain off excess fat. Return chicken to pan and pour sauce evenly over pieces. Bring to boil; cover, reduce heat and simmer 45 minutes, turning chicken occasionally. Serve with sauce over boiled rice or noodles. Makes 3 to 4 servings.

STUFFED EGGS

6 hard-cooked eggs, peeled   1 tablespoon minced parsley
1 tablespoon mayonnaise   1 teaspoon dry mustard
1 tablespoon **KIKKOMAN** Soy Sauce   Dash paprika

Cut eggs in halves crosswise in a decorative sawtooth pattern; gently remove yolks. Mix yolks with mayonnaise, soy sauce, parsley and mustard. Refill whites with yolk mixture and garnish with paprika. Makes 12 stuffed eggs.

Pork and Lamb

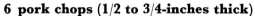

GLAZED PORK CHOPS

  6 **pork chops (1/2 to 3/4-inches thick)**
  2 **tablespoons shortening or oil**
 1/2 **cup KIKKOMAN Teriyaki Sauce**
 1/2 **cup apple juice**
  1 **tablespoon cornstarch**
  1 **tablespoon water**

Brown pork chops on both sides in shortening; pour off excess fat. Combine teriyaki sauce and apple juice; pour over chops. Cover, reduce heat and simmer until chops are tender, about 30 minutes, turning occasionally. Meanwhile, blend together cornstarch and water. Remove chops and stir cornstarch mixture into sauce. Bring to boil and cook until sauce thickens. Return chops and coat thoroughly with sauce. Serve immediately. Makes 4 to 6 servings.

BRAISED ISLAND PORK

1-1/2 **pounds lean boneless pork**
  3 **tablespoons flour (about)**
  1 **tablespoon shortening or oil**
  1 **clove garlic, crushed**
 1/2 **cup KIKKOMAN Teriyaki Sauce**
 1/2 **cup water**
 1/3 **cup light brown sugar, firmly packed**
 1/4 **cup cider vinegar**
 1/4 **pound carrots, thinly sliced**
  1 **medium onion, cut in squares**
  2 **tablespoons cornstarch**
  2 **tablespoons water**
  1 **medium green pepper, cut in squares**

Cut pork into 1-inch cubes; coat thoroughly with flour. Heat shortening in Dutch oven or large heavy frying pan; add pork and garlic and cook until pork is thoroughly brown. Stir in teriyaki sauce, 1/2 cup water, brown sugar and vinegar; bring to boil. Cover, reduce heat and simmer 45 minutes, stirring occasionally. Add carrots and simmer 10 minutes. Add onions and simmer 5 minutes longer. Meanwhile, blend cornstarch and 2 tablespoons water; stir into sauce with green pepper. Bring to boil and cook only until sauce is thickened. Makes 4 to 6 servings.

59

PORK CUTLETS MILANO STYLE

    4 pork tenderloin patties or pork cutlets
      (about 1/2-inch thick)
1/8 teaspoon garlic powder
    4 teaspoons KIKKOMAN Soy Sauce
1/4 cup flour (about)
    1 egg, beaten
    1 tablespoon water
    1 cup dry bread crumbs
1/4 cup salad oil

Slice cutlets horizontally in half, being careful not to cut all the way through; flatten and score edges to prevent curling. Sprinkle garlic powder and 4 teaspoons soy sauce on cutlets; let stand 5 minutes. Coat cutlets with flour. Combine egg and water. Dip floured cutlets into egg mixture, then into bread crumbs. Heat oil in frying pan, add cutlets and brown and cook on both sides until meat is tender. Makes 4 servings.

SWEET-SOUR PORK

1/2 pound pork tender loin, cut into bite-size pieces
  1 tablespoon KIKKOMAN Soy Sauce
  2 teaspoons sake (Japanese cooking wine) or dry white wine
1/2 teaspoon grated fresh ginger root
1/4 cup cornstarch (about)
    Vegetable oil for frying
  1 can (8-1/4 oz.) sliced pineapple, drained
  3 tablespoons salad oil
  1 clove garlic, crushed
  1 small onion, cut in eighths
  2 shiitake (dried Japanese forest mushrooms), softened and cut in halves
  1 can (4 oz.) sliced bamboo shoot, drained
  1 small carrot, thinly sliced
1/2 cup condensed beef bouillon
1/4 cup sugar
  2 teaspoons KIKKOMAN Soy Sauce
  2 teaspoons catsup

1 tablespoon cornstarch
1/4 cup vinegar
2 tablespoons frozen green peas, optional

Season pork tenderloin pieces with 1 tablespoon soy sauce, sake and ginger. Coat thoroughly with cornstarch. Heat oil in deep electric frying pan or deep fat fryer to about 360°F. Add pork pieces and fry until golden brown and pork is thoroughly cooked. Drain off excess fat; keep warm. Cut each pineapple slice into 6 pieces. Heat 3 tablespoons salad oil in wok. Add garlic, onion, mushrooms, bamboo shoots and carrot. Stir-fry until vegetables are tender, yet crisp. Stir in bouillon, water; stir into vegetable mixture. Bring to boil and cook only until sauce thickens. Add vinegar, pork, pineapple and peas, stirring to combine. Serve immediately. Makes 4 servings.

SPARERIBS HAWAIIAN

3 to 4 pounds spareribs
1 can (1 lb., 4 oz.) sliced pineapple
1/2 cup KIKKOMAN Soy Sauce
1/4 cup catsup

2 tablespoons brown sugar, firmly packed
1 clove garlic, crushed

Cut ribs into serving pieces. Place in shallow baking pan, meaty side down. Bake in 450° oven 30 minutes. Remove from oven and drain off excess fat. Reduce oven temperature to 350°. Drain pineapple, reserving 3/4 cup syrup. Combine reserved syrup with soy sauce, catsup, brown sugar and garlic; pour evenly over ribs. Cover pan with aluminum foil; bake 1 hour. Remove foil; turn ribs over and place pineapple slices on ribs. Brush ribs and pineapple with sauce. Return to oven for 15 minutes, or until pineapple is hot and ribs are glazed. To serve, spoon sauce over ribs and pineapple. Makes 4 to 6 servings.

SWEET-SOUR SPARERIBS

3 to 4 pounds pork spareribs
3/4 cup orange marmalade

1/2 cup KIKKOMAN Teriyaki Sauce
1/2 cup cider vinegar

Cut ribs into serving portions. Place in foil-lined broiler pan or shallow roasting pan, meaty side down. Bake in 450° oven 30 minutes. Remove from oven; reduce temperature to 350°. Drain fat from pan. Return to oven and bake 30 minutes. Meanwhile, combine marmalade, teriyaki sauce and vinegar. Turn ribs over; brush thoroughly with sauce. Pour remaining sauce over ribs. Bake 30 minutes longer, or until tender, basting occasionally. If desired, spoon sauce over ribs before serving. Makes 4 servings.

BARBECUED SPARERIBS

4 pounds pork spareribs, cut into serving pieces
1 cup KIKKOMAN Soy Sauce
2 tablespoons cornstarch
1/2 cup catsup
1/2 cup water
2 tablespoons vinegar
2 tablespoons KIKKOMAN Soy Sauce
1 tablespoon brown sugar, firmly packed
1/4 teaspoon chili powder
1/4 teaspoon celery seed

Place spareribs in pan; cover with water and bring to a boil. Simmer about 20 minutes, or until almost tender. Meanwhile, blend together 1 cup soy sauce and cornstarch. Drain spareribs and pat dry with paper toweling. While ribs are still hot, brush with soy sauce mixture, allow to dry and brush again. Repeat procedure until all of soy sauce mixture is used. (Takes about 40 minutes.) Meanwhile, combine catsup, water, vinegar, 2 tablespoons soy sauce, brown sugar, chili powder and celery seed in saucepan; bring to boil. Place spareribs on grill over hot coals; brush with barbecue sauce. Cook about 20 to 30 minutes, turning and brushing frequently with sauce. Serve remaining sauce with ribs. Makes 4 to 6 servings.

NOTE: Using all of the soy sauce-cornstarch mixture is the secret to the success of this recipe. It is time-consuming but worth it!

LAZY-DAY LAMB PILAF

1 pound boneless lamb stew meat
1 tablespoon butter or margarine
7 tablespoons KIKKOMAN Teriyaki Sauce
2 tablespoons onion soup mix
2 cups boiling water
3/4 cup uncooked long-grain rice
2 tablespoons chopped pimiento

Cut lamb into 3/4-inch cubes. Melt butter in frying pan with cover. Add lamb and brown. Stir in 3 tablespoons teriyaki sauce, cover and simmer 50 to 60 minutes, or until lamb is tender (stir occasionally and, if necessary, add some water). Meanwhile, combine soup mix, boiling water, rice, 1/4 cup teriyaki sauce and pimiento in 1-1/2 quart baking dish. Cover and bake in 350° oven 25 to 30 minutes, or until rice is tender. Remove lamb from sauce and add to hot rice. Toss gently to combine. Makes 4 servings.

64

LAMB SPARERIBS

    3 **pounds lamb spareribs**
1/2 **cup KIKKOMAN Teriyaki Sauce**
    2 **tablespoons orange marmalade**
    1 **clove garlic, crushed**

Trim off as much fat as possible from spareribs. Place in baking pan; bake in 325° oven 1 hour. Meanwhile, combine teriyaki sauce with marmalade and garlic.

Drain off fat from pan; pour sauce over ribs and continue baking 30 minutes, brushing occasionally with sauce. Makes 4 to 6 servings.

BROILED LAMB CHOPS

1/4 **cup KIKKOMAN Soy Sauce**   1/8 **teaspoon garlic powder**
   2 **tablespoons dry white wine**   6 **to 8 shoulder lamb chops**

Combine soy sauce, wine and garlic in shallow dish. Dip both sides of lamb chops into soy sauce mixture. Broil to desired degree of doneness, brushing occasionally with sauce. Makes 3 to 4 servings.

Sea Food

SEAFOOD AND VEGETABLE TEMPURA

Allow at least 4 shrimps and 6 pieces of other ingredients of your choice for each serving.

Fresh shrimp or prawns (21 to 25 count per pound), shelled, butterflied and deveined, leaving tail on
Fish fillets, cut in 1-1/2 ×2-inch pieces
Green peppers, cut in 1-1/2 ×2-inch pieces
Celery, cut in 1/2 ×2-inch pieces
Sweet potatoes or carrots, peeled and sliced diagonally in 1/4-inch thick slices
Eggplant or zucchini, unpeeled and sliced in 1/4-inch thick slices
Large fresh mushrooms, sliced in 1/4-inch thick slices

Drain seafoods and vegetables thoroughly on paper towels; arrange on large platter. Pour vegetable oil for frying at least 4 inches deep into electric frying pan, electric wok, or deep, wide frying pan; heat to 375°.
(Batter)

1 large-size egg
1-1/4 cups ice-cold water
2 cups sifted cake flour

Beat egg thoroughly with wire wisk or hand rotary beater (not electric). Blend in water. Sprinkle all of flour evenly over liquid. With same wire wisk or beater, stir in flour quickly only until flour is moistened and large lumps disappear. Batter should be very lumpy. Do not stir batter after it is mixed. To fry shrimp, hold one at a time by the tail and dip into batter. Drain off excess batter slightly and slide shrimp gently into hot oil. Repeat with 3 or 4 more shrimp. Fry shrimp about 1 minute, turn over and fry 1 minute longer, or until lightly golden brown. Dip and fry other ingredients in the same manner as shrimp. Drain tempura on paper towels or on wire rack over cake pan. Skim off pieces of cooked batter from oil with wire strainer.

Tempura Dipping Sauce:

1-1/2 cups hot water
1/2 cup KIKKOMAN Soy Sauce
1/4 teaspoon grated fresh ginger, if desired
1/8 teaspoon MSG

Combine all ingredients and pour into small individual bowls. Serve with tempura. Enough sauce for about 6 servings.

SHRIMP-CURL KABOBS

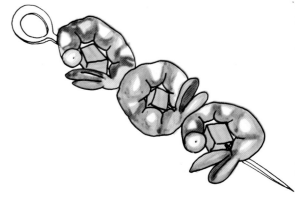

  24 **canned pineapple chunks**
        (most of 13-1/4 oz. can)
  24 **large raw shrimps (about 1 lb.),**
        peeled and deveined
1/3 **cup KIKKOMAN Teriyaki Sauce**
1/4 **cup water**
   1 **tablespoon lemon juice**
   2 **teaspoons cornstarch**

Place 1 pineapple chunk in curve of each shrimp, then thread 3 shrimps on each skewer (at least 6 inches long). Combine teriyaki sauce, water, lemon juice and cornstarch in saucepan. Bring mixture to boil, stirring 1 minute. Remove from heat and brush both sides of kabobs with sauce. Broil 5 inches below preheated broiler or over hot coals 3 to 5 minutes on each side. Brush kabobs again with sauce. Makes 4 servings.

67

Tempura— A "Japanese" Dish Imported from the West

by Shigeru Otsuka

When we in Japan treat Americans or other foreigners to a tempura dinner they are very pleased, but on the other hand we are kept busy answering their questions. This is because, when eating tempura, most people keep asking, "What is this? And what is this one here?"

When we come to think about it, we find that this problem arises because the Japanese use almost anything to make tempura. Fish, prawns, crabs, shellfish, beans, green vegetables, potatoes—all make delicious tempura.

So it can be said that the ingredients for tempura are unlimited. And if the ingredients are unlimited, so are the questions. Now as most of my American friends are nutritionists they are not content when I just tell them the name of the fish or vegetable. They want to know what family or variety they belong to and what the scientific names are. In Japan we have a saying that "If you eat tempura you will become eloquent." I always fancied myself reasonably eloquent, but there has been more than one party where I was completely at a loss for an answer, and this because of tempura.

In Europe, deep frying as a way of cooking was developed in the days of the Roman Empire. It is said that the splendid dishes which were served at the banquets of the Roman Emperors were mostly deep fried.

In Japan, people had been using fat in small quantities since time immemorial, but it was only in the sixteenth century, after Japan had got in touch with Western civilization, that fat was used in large quantities as a means of cooking. The Spaniards and Portuguese had come to Japan chiefly to spread Christianity, but they also brought various foodstuffs, to which they treated the military ruler of Japan and the local lords as well as the common people. In fact the word tempura is said to be a corruption of either a Portuguese or a Spanish word.

Whatever the origin of the word may have been, tempura seems to have gained wide popularity in a short time. Shortly afterwards, the country was isolated and remained cut off from the outside world for nearly 300 years. During that time tempura cooking was improved little by little until it had been turned into a thoroughly Japanese dish, so much so that today most Japanese themselves are amazed when told that tempura was originally imported from the West.

Tempura is a first-rate food, in point of taste, nutritional value, and, happily, price as well, since you can choose the ingredients to fit your taste and pocketbook. The chef of the Imperial Household, Tokuzo Akiyama, who has a world-wide reputation as a master of Western cuisine, has praised tempura as "an international dish that will be a feast for anybody, no matter what his nationality may be. . . . I rather doubt that we will be able in the next few generations to create another dish that can compare with tempura in terms of quality and deliciousness."

The Japanese place a high value on the visual attractiveness of their food, a tendency which is evident in tempura. The pink tail of a prawn that peeps from the batter coating, greens that have been coated only on one side so that their colors are enhanced, all add interest to each piece of tempura. This elegant dish has little in common with the greasy fried Western food that its ancestor must have been.

The ingredient, however, that brings the taste of tempura to perfection is the tempura sauce in which we dip the tempura. You can eat tempura with salt only and it will taste good, but when you eat it with shoyu it will be even more delicious. The flavor of shoyu together with the flavor of oil bring forth the characteristic tempura deliciousness. However, shoyu has a high salt content, so if you dip your tempura into undiluted shoyu it will taste too salty. Therefore other ingredients are added to the tempura sauce to retain the merits of shoyu and obtain a delicate, mild taste at the same time. Grated radish is one of these ingredients, and the lipase it contains has the additional advantage of aiding digestion.

Indeed, in tempura the beauty and aroma of the Japanese cuisine are brought to perfection. However, some Americans and Europeans who especially like fried meat dishes have difficulty appreciating really good tempura. "Why do the Japanese make such a fuss about fried leaves? Why don't you fry pork or beef?" I have often been asked. The Japanese "use almost anything for tempura" but they have not yet tried beef or pork. This is simply because it does not suit the Japanese taste. Once a completely foreign dish to the Japanese, tempura now enjoys an ever-increasing popularity among Westerners as one of the most typical Japanese dishes. This is so only because the Japanese adopted the Western way of cooking but not Western ingredients. One or the other had to be done without.

PRAWNS IN THE SHELL

    1 **pound large raw shrimp or prawns**
    2 **tablespoons sake (Japanese cooking wine) or dry white wine**
1/2 **teaspoon grated fresh ginger root**
1/4 **cup salad oil**
    2 **tablespoons coarsely chopped green onion**
    1 **teaspoon coarsely chopped fresh ginger root**
    1 **clove garlic, chopped**
    2 **small red chili peppers, coarsely chopped**
    3 **tablespoons catsup**
    2 **tablespoons KIKKOMAN Soy Sauce**
    1 **tablespoon sugar**
1/2 **teaspoon cornstarch**

Wash and devein shrimp. (Do not shell.) Cut diagonally into halves. Sprinkle 1 tablespoon sake and grated ginger over shrimp. Heat oil in frying pan; add shrimp and saute until completely pink or red. Stir in green onions, ginger, garlic and chili peppers and cook only until green onions are tender. Combine catsup, soy sauce, sugar, remaining sake and cornstarch; pour into pan, bring to boil, and cook only until sauce thickens. Serve immediately. Makes 4 servings.

SCALLOP CASSEROLE

    1 **can (4 oz.) sliced mushrooms**
    1 **pound sea scallops**
    1 **tablespoon butter or margarine**
    1 **can (10-1/2 oz.) condensed cream of mushroom soup**
1/2 **cup sour cream**
1/4 **cup water**
    1 **tablespoon KIKKOMAN Soy Sauce**
    1 **tablespoon lemon juice**
1/2 **cup shredded Cheddar cheese**

Drain mushrooms; reserve liquid. Cut scallops into halves. Melt butter in frying pan, add scallops and saute 2 or 3 minutes. Stir in reserved mushroom liquid and simmer 10 minutes. Pour into baking dish. Stir in cream of mushroom soup, sour cream, water, soy sauce and lemon juice. Sprinkle cheese over casserole. Bake in 450° oven until cheese is lightly browned, about 15 minutes. Makes 4 servings.

TUNA CASSEROLE

> 1-1/2 **cups elbow macaroni**
> 1/4 **cup butter or margarine**
> 1/4 **cup flour**
> 1-3/4 **cups water**
> 2 **tablespoons KIKKOMAN Soy Sauce**
> 1 **cup shredded Cheddar cheese**
> **Dash black pepper**
> 1 **can (about 7 oz.) tuna, drained and flaked**
> 1/2 **cup finely chopped green pepper**

Cook macaroni in boiling salted water until tender, yet firm. Drain. Melt butter in saucepan; blend in flour. Add 1-3/4 cups water and soy sauce all at once; stir until well blended. Simmer until sauce thickens, stirring constantly. Remove from heat and blend in black pepper and 3/4 of cheese. Combine tuna, macaroni and green pepper in ungreased 1-1/2 quart baking dish. Stir in cheese sauce. Sprinkle remaining cheese over top. Bake in 425° oven until top is golden brown, about 15 minutes. Makes 4 servings.

70

Sauces

ALL-PURPOSE SEAFOOD SAUCE

1 cup tomato catsup	1 tablespoon KIKKOMAN Soy Sauce
1/3 cup lemon juice	1 tablespoon prepared horseradish
1 tablespoon minced onion	1/2 teaspoon anise seed, crushed

Thoroughly blend catsup, lemon juice, onion, soy sauce, horseradish and anise seed. Cover and refrigerate several hours. Makes about 1–1/2 cups sauce.

BASIC TERIYAKI SAUCE

1/2 cup KIKKOMAN Soy Sauce	1/2 teaspoon ground ginger
1/4 cup dry white wine	1/4 teaspoon garlic powder
2 tablespoons sugar	

Blend together soy sauce, wine, sugar, ginger and garlic. Makes about 3/4 cup.

For Beef Teriyaki:

Pour sauce over tender steaks and marinate about 20 minutes, or pour over less tender steaks, such as chuck or round steaks and marinate 1 to 2 hours at room temperature or overnight in refrigerator. Broil or grill to desired degree of doneness.

For Chicken Teriyaki:

Pour sauce over a 3-pound cut-up broiler-fryer and marinate 1 to 2 hours in refrigerator. Bake in 325° oven about 1 hour, turning and basting occasionally with sauce.

For Fish Teriyaki:

Prepare teriyaki sauce (above) in saucepan. Combine 1/4 cup water with 1 tablespoon cornstarch. Bring teriyaki sauce to boil, gradually stir in cornstarch mixture and cook, stirring constantly, until sauce thickens. Serve over grilled or broiled steaks of halibut, salmon or red snapper.

WESTERN BARBECUE SAUCE

    1/2 **cup KIKKOMAN Soy Sauce**
    1/2 **cup catsup**
    1/4 **cup wine**
    1/4 **cup butter or margarine, melted**
      1 **small onion, finely chopped**
      2 **tablespoons sugar**
    1/4 **teaspoon chili powder**
    1/4 **teaspoon black pepper**
      1 **clove garlic, crushed**

Thoroughly blend together all ingredients in saucepan; heat to boiling. Remove from heat and brush or spoon onto meat while broiling or barbecuing. Makes about 1–1/2 cups.

ZESTY STEAK SAUCE

    1/4 **cup finely chopped green onions**
      1 **tablespoon butter or margarine**
    1/3 **cup KIKKOMAN Teriyaki Sauce**
    1/4 **cup catsup**
      2 **tablespoons dry mustard**
    1/4 **teaspoon black pepper**

Saute onions in butter until tender. Stir in teriyaki sauce, catsup, mustard and pepper; bring to boil. Remove from heat and serve over broiled or grilled steaks. Makes about 2/3 cup.

ASPARAGUS WITH PEANUT BUTTER-SHOYU SAUCE

      1 **pound fresh asparagus**
    1/4 **cup KIKKOMAN Soy Sauce**
      2 **tablespoons peanut butter**

Cook asparagus in boiling salted water until tender; drain. Meanwhile, blend soy sauce, a little at a time, into peanut butter, mixing thoroughly. Serve with asparagus. Makes 4 servings.

TANGY DIPPING SAUCE FOR VEGETABLES

  1/2 cup KIKKOMAN Soy Sauce
  1/4 cup fresh lime juice

Combine soy sauce with lime juice. Serve as dipping sauce for raw or cooked vegetable pieces, for appetizers. Makes 3/4 cup sauce.

QUICK AND ZESTY TOPPING FOR VEGETABLES

  1/2 cup mayonnaise
  ** 1 teaspoon KIKKOMAN Soy Sauce**
  1/2 teaspoon lemon juice
  **   Dash paprika**

Combine mayonnaise, soy sauce, lemon juice and paprika until well blended. Pour over hot, cooked broccoli or asparagus spears. Makes 1/2 cup.

Miscellaneous

HAWAIIAN HAM STEAK

1 fully cooked ham slice, 1 inch thick
Whole cloves
1 can (8-1/4 oz.) sliced pineapple
1 tablespoon brown sugar, firmly packed
2 teaspoons KIKKOMAN Soy Sauce

Score edges of ham in diamond pattern; insert cloves into fat. Drain pineapple, reserving 3 tablespoons syrup. Combine syrup with brown sugar and soy sauce. Brush both sides of ham with sauce; place in shallow baking dish. Bake in 325° oven 30 minutes, brushing occasionally with sauce. Add pineapple slices during final 10 minutes of baking. Makes 4 servings.

CORN-ON-THE-COB KIKKOMAN

1/2 cup (1/4 lb.) soft butter or margarine
1 tablespoon KIKKOMAN Soy Sauce
1/2 teaspoon tarragon leaves
6 ears fresh corn

Thoroughly blend together butter, soy sauce and tarragon. Husk corn. Lay each ear on piece of foil large enough to wrap around it; spread ears generously with seasoned butter. Wrap foil around corn and seal edges. Cook on grill 3 inches from coals 20 to 30 minutes, turning frequently. Serve immediately.
OR: Place wrapped ears of corn on baking sheet. Bake in 325° oven 30 minutes.
NOTE: Butter-soy mixture may also be spread on hot boiled corn. Makes 6 servings.

CELERY KIKKOMAN

4 stalks celery
1/2 cup KIKKOMAN Soy Sauce

Cut celery stalks into 1-inch pieces. Pour soy sauce over celery; stir. Marinate in refrigerator 24 hours. Remove from soy sauce and serve as a snack.
NOTE: For best results, do not marinate longer than 24 hours.

74

Japanese Cooking

NIGIRI SUSHI

   1/2 **recipe sushi-meshi (seasoned rice for sushi)**
     6 **medium-sized raw shrimp**
   1/2 **cup rice wine vinegar**
     2 **tablespoons sugar**
   1/2 **teaspoon salt**
   1/2 **pound filleted red snapper, in one piece**
   1/2 **pound filleted striped bass, in one piece**
   1/2 **pound filleted tuna, in one piece**
     1 **tablespoon wasabi (green horseradish powder)**
     1 **tablespoon water**

Prepare sushi-meshi according to directions; cool to room temperature. Meanwhile, insert a bamboo skewer lengthwise through each shrimp, to prevent curling during cooking. Drop shrimp into boiling, salted water and cook about 5 minutes. Drain and cool to room temperature. Remove skewers; shell and devein, being careful to leave tails on. Butterfly each shrimp by slitting lengthwise on underside, almost to the back. Combine vinegar, sugar and salt; add shrimp and marinate about 30 minutes. Remove shrimp and drain; reserve vinegar mixture. Blend wasabi with water, let stand 15 minutes. Slice red snapper and striped bass crosswise at an angle into 1/4-inch thick slices. Cut tuna in same fashion into 1/2-inch thick slices.

To assemble:

    Dip fingers into reserved vinegar mixture and pick up about 1 tablespoon sushi-meshi. Shape into an oblong piece. Dab a small amount of wasabi paste inside each shrimp and down the center of each piece of fish. Holding the rice in one hand and shrimp or fish in the other, press the two together (shrimp or fish should completely cover top of rice.) Serve nigiri sushi with soy sauce. Makes about 6 servings.

76

CHIRASHI SUSHI

  1/2 **recipe sushi-meshi (seasoned rice for sushi)**
    4 **medium-sized shiitake (dried forest mushrooms)**
    1 **can (10 oz.) chirashi-sushi-no-moto (prepared vegetables for chirashi-sushi)**
    2 **tablespoons KIKKOMAN Soy Sauce**
    2 **tablespoons sake (Japanese rice wine)**
    2 **tablespoons sugar**
    6 **medium-sized shrimp**
  1/2 **cup rice wine vinegar**
    2 **tablespoons sugar**
  1/2 **teaspoon salt**
    3 **eggs, beaten**
    1 **tablespoon water**
  1/2 **teaspoon salt**
    1 **can (3-1/4 oz.) crabmeat, drained and flaked**
      several sheets ajitsuke nori (seasoned dried seaweed)
    2 **pieces beni-shoga (red pickled ginger)**

Prepare sushi-meshi according to directions; cool to room temperature. Soften shiitake in 2 cups water for 30 minutes. Remove from water and squeeze out liquid; reserve mushroom liquid. Remove and discard stems, cut mushrooms into thin strips. Measure 1/2 cup of the mushroom liquid into saucepan; stir in soy sauce, sake and 2 tablespoons sugar. Add mushrooms and chirashi-sushi-no-moto. Cook until well seasoned. Drain thoroughly and cool to room temperature. Meanwhile, insert a bamboo skewer lengthwise through each shrimp, to prevent curling during cooking. Drop shrimp into boiling, salted water and cook about 5 minutes. Drain and cool to room temperature. Remove skewers; shell and devein shrimp, being careful to leave tails on. Butterfly each shrimp by slitting lengthwise on underside, almost to the back. Combine vinegar, 2 tablespoons sugar and 1/2 teaspoon salt; add shrimp and marinate about 30 minutes. Remove shrimp and drain on absorbent paper. Blend eggs with water and 1/2 teaspoon salt. Pour into hot greased 10-inch frying pan; tip back and forth to spread eggs. Cook until omelet is firm on bottom, turn over and cook until eggs are firm. Carefully remove from pan in one piece onto cutting board. Cut into strips or squares. Slice nori into fine shreds and beni-shoga into thin slivers.

To assemble:

  Gently but thoroughly toss together sushi-meshi, chirashi-sushi-no-moto mixture and crabmeat. Divide into 6 equal portions and firmly pack into 6 individual bowls. Top with shrimp and egg; garnish with nori and beni-shoga. Makes 6 servings.

SUIMONO (Clear Soup)

    1 **bag (3/4 oz.) dashi-no-moto**
    3 **cups water**
    1 **tablespoon KIKKOMAN Soy Sauce**
        Fresh spinach leaves, cut in bite-size pieces
1/2 **cake tofu (soybean curd), cut in 1/2-inch cubes**
        Thin pieces of lemon peel

Add dashi-no-moto to water; bring to boil. Reduce heat and simmer 10 minutes. Remove from heat and stir in soy sauce. Serve in individual bowls and garnish with spinach, tofu and lemon peel. Makes 4 to 6 servings.
NOTE: Regular-strength chicken broth may be substituted for water and dashi-no-moto; reduce soy sauce to 2 teaspoons.

78

UDON

> 1 **package (1 lb.) udon (Japanese wide flat noodles)***
> 2 **bags (3/4 oz. each) dashi-no-moto**
> 6 **cups water**
> 2 **tablespoons KIKKOMAN Soy Sauce**
> 1/2 **teaspoon sugar**
> **Finely chopped green onions**
> **Sliced hard-cooked eggs, if desired**

Cook udon in boiling, salted water until noodles are very soft, stirring occasionally. Drain and keep warm. Add bags of dashi-no-moto to 6 cups water; bring to boil. Reduce heat and simmer 10 minutes. Remove from heat and stir in soy sauce and sugar. Divide udon into individual bowls; pour hot broth over noodles and garnish with green onions and eggs. Makes 4 to 6 servings.
* If udon is not available, egg noodles may be substituted.

Postscript

Shoyu. Perfected over the centuries in Japan, and the one indispensable seasoning for all Japanese foods for centuries.

Now shoyu is becoming the indispensable seasoning for foods of all lands. Universally, people are discovering shoyu and they are devising new ways to use shoyu. Also, they are finding that their old favorite foods have hidden goodness, flavor nuances that were just waiting to be brought out by shoyu.

We at Kikkoman are doing our best to help the world make the discovery. And we feel genuinely happy that our business consists of helping people to expand their enjoyment of food. We feel that when we succeed, our new customers have not merely substituted one food for another; they have found a way to make virtually everything they eat taste better.

Our efforts to introduce shoyu to America have seen three stages since 1949 when we resumed exporting after World War Two.

The first stage was one of sales expansion. This stage culminated in the establishment of Kikkoman International Inc. in San Francisco.

The second stage saw Kikkoman International establishing branches in Los Angeles, New York, and Chicago. Sales volume rose greatly, but so did shipping costs, both for the wheat and soybeans that we shipped from America to Japan, and for the finished bottled shoyu that we shipped from Japan. To hold down such costs on at least one end, we began packing shoyu and producing teriyaki sauce at Leslie Foods Inc. in Oakland.

More and more American consumers came to use Kikkoman, so many that finally we built a production plant in the United States to serve the American market. This marked the end of the third stage and the beginning of the fourth. It is also, I believe, the first major step toward demonstrating the true potential of Kikkoman Shoyu as a food product of world-wide value and appeal.

This book was intended as an introduction to Japan's brewed shoyu. I hope it has served to deepen your interest in and understanding of Japan and Japanese food, and that it will give you a fuller appreciation of the goodness and versatility of shoyu, in both Japanese and American foods.

Saheiji Mogi
President, Kikkoman Shoyu Co., Ltd.